Breaking Into The Media

- A Journalist's Guide to Publicity

SANDRA COFFEY

Copyright © 2021 Sandra Coffey All rights reserved.

No part of this book may be reproduced, or stored in a retrieval system, or transmitted in any form or by any means, electronic, mechanical, photocopying, recording, or otherwise, without express written permission of the author. Requests to the author for permission should be addressed to the following email: solassandra@gmail.com

Limitation of liability/disclaimer of warranty: While the author has used her best efforts in preparing this book, she makes no representations or warranties with respect to the accuracy or completeness of the contents of this document and specifically disclaims any implied warranties of merchantability or fitness for particular purpose. No warranty may be created or extended by sales representatives, promoters, or written sales materials.

The advice and strategies contained herein may not be suitable for your situation. You should consult with a professional where appropriate. The author shall not be liable for any loss of profit or any other commercial damages, including but not limited to special, incidental, consequential, or other damages.

Due to the dynamic nature of the Internet, certain website information contained in this publication may have changed. The author and publisher make no representations to the current accuracy of the web information shared.

ISBN: 9798732106008

Cover design: Phycel Designs

Author Photo: Julia Dunin Photography

CONTENTS

1	Introduction – A Breakfast Tradition That Began A Media Career	3
2	Getting To The Starting Blocks	13
3	The Cake That Made The Headlines	28
4	The Routes You Can Take	36
5	The Ingredients You Need	55
6	Inside The Newsroom	64
7	Generating Ideas	84
8	Broadcast Media At Different Times Of The Day	98
9	Supplements – The Untapped Gem of Publicity	116
10	Classified Adverts – More Than Lonely-Hearts Column	132
11	Why You Don't Hear Back	138
12	Types of Press Release	155
13	The Press Release – Structure And What To Include	163
14	The Pitch Email	181
15	Photographs	215
16	The Interview	234
17	Launch Time	247
18	Dealing With Emotions And Media Publicity	267
19	Conclusion and Media Publicity Checklist	277

About the Author

How To Work With Sandra

Acknowledgements

CHAPTER 1 - INTRODUCTION

A BREAKFAST TRADITION THAT BEGAN A MEDIA CAREER

It's 10am on a Saturday morning in a busy kitchen located on a farm in the west of Ireland. And while most families are settling down to breakfast and catching up on each other's week, in the house I grew up in, the news was an integral part of our morning. As was the weather report! It was natural for my siblings and I to stay silent while the headlines were being read out. Then conversations would resume again and be intermittently disrupted by a news story one or all of us wanted to hear. As a 10-year-old, I loved the feeling of having the outside world play a major part in our weekend mornings and in our conversations. That feeling of being almost like an adult for a while. I remember talking about politics, sport, fashion, and world leaders at the kitchen table, all prompted by a news story we heard or read. After the news came the weather and after that came the death notices which sadly sometimes were more important than any news headline as my parents waited to hear the funeral details of someone they knew.

Why do I share this with you?

I share this with you because although I didn't know it then but looking back now, news was a normal part of my day. It was a habit my parents had and were passing on unwittingly. They knew about presenters, shows, segments. They knew about the beats journalists had, the presenters that were destined for great things, the journalists who weren't afraid to say things out straight.

I quickly discovered that this wasn't the norm especially when I started visiting friends' houses. This undoubtedly had an impact on my decision to become a writer and journalist. And to this day, I still make news a part of my routine. Why? Because that is how you become and stay relevant and get media publicity. And because I love knowing what is making the news! Making the media a part of your routine and not something to tap into when you need to get featured is by far the most rewarding way you will go about your publicity journey. Because, as I always say this is a journey and one you need to be invested in from the start. So, turn on that podcast you want to be featured on, read that blogger's post, tune into that news programme, go pick up that newspaper or magazine and start to get familiar with what they do. This is the best place to start! I recommend you do this before you put together your pitch for publicity.

Media publicity is a gamechanger with longevity - Only when done with intention

Getting publicity isn't simple and run from anyone who tells you it is. Yes, you can get lucky when your story, angle, timing, having a good spokesperson and the right journalist to tell your story are all aligned. But this isn't often the case. It rarely is. You have to work at it and be strategic with your efforts. You need to build your media presence from the ground up and this can only be achieved by knowing the media. Also, keep in mind it is competitive, and journalists are being pitched to constantly.

But don't get disheartened! In fact, this is the one thing I help many people with when they ask for my help. They already feel unworthy of media attention simply because the journalist never replied to their pitch. They feel that this is going to be a lot of work. I am here to tell you that you are worthy, and I will show you ways to make this process easier to do so you can start to feel less overwhelmed and ultimately get featured. But you must first understand that it takes time, dedication, and an interest in the news cycle.

You're here because you want to learn how to generate publicity consistently, or you are starting from scratch and want to get on the right path to knowing what you need and how to deliver it. Whatever path you are on, the methods I will share will help you become the one that gets featured and, builds strong relationships with journalists which will ultimately lead you to growing your reputation and expertise in your field.

Same mistakes again and again

I have written this book because, for many years (close to 17), people have pitched to me, whether successfully or unsuccessfully, and I've seen the same mistakes happen over and over. This book is all about giving you the viewpoint of a journalist, who is the person you need to convince to cover your story. Too many people assume a lack of a response from a journalist means the journalist was too busy to read their press release or their story wasn't good enough. This isn't necessarily the case. Every journalist wants to be the next one to find a hit story. You need to make it easy for them to find it. With the right story and an engaging person to tell it, media publicity can do amazing things. I know this because I've seen first-hand how this can happen. Later in this book, I will show you how you can avoid making the mistakes that can make even the best story fall flat.

My first years

I started my career before social media existed. In a way, I feel lucky that I did. I had to build my communication and people skills and not be afraid to get a door slammed in my face (literally) or have someone scream at me and then bang the phone down. Then, there is the other side where people went out of their way to help me get the information I needed. One builds up skills and finds resolve at times when things are tough. You get up after another door is closed and work harder to get the story or the number you need of someone so you can start to gather details. We called people on the phone back then! We looked at newspapers in their paper format spread out over the floor. We cut out articles in magazines. We admired photoshoots by other photographers and tried to learn from them.

Then there are the stories that stop you in your tracks. The times as a journalist when I sat down to interview a parent who had just lost a son or daughter in horrific circumstances. The days were never boring, and this is still true albeit social media has made it a lot easier to contact people. When I talk about my first years in journalism to people, they look at me in total surprise. I got story pitches sent in on a fax machine (yes!) and through the regular post. At a set time every week, a member of the news team would wait by the fax to receive the crime report from the police. Sometimes, a story began from one-line that was written on a page and dropped through the front door letterbox of the newspaper. And yes, the job of a journalist was much harder then. You had to put in a lot more groundwork to clarify details and develop a story. Despite all this, if the story stood up and needed to be told, it didn't matter what format these details arrived in.

Social media has made it much easier both for the journalist and for you the person pitching your story. I deal with this in more detail later as there are dos and don'ts that I believe you should be aware of when drumming up the interest of a journalist online.

This book's approach

This book details what it takes to get the attention of someone who sits at a desk in a busy newsroom or magazine, radio, or television office, as I did for 17 years. There are lots of good academic books on media relations out there. This isn't one of them. Writing an academic book didn't feel right to me. This is a hands-on guide to get you from the stage of not knowing where to start or having experienced many false starts to ultimately gaining the confidence to tell your story and get the media attention you deserve.

I am pulling back the curtain and showing you inside the newsroom. For me, understanding how a newsroom works is essential to building a relationship with a journalist. However, this type of information is not taught in PR courses which puts the PR professional on a steep learning curve from the get-go. Whether you are a PR professional or not, this book will give you insights into how the newsroom works so you can start to think more about what a journalist needs and when he/she needs it.

Before I go any further, I just want to say that I have often heard that social media will result in the death of newspapers and traditional publishing. I'm here to tell you that traditional media is not dead, far from it! It is just in a different format and social media has hastened its journey down a new road, a road a lot of us saw coming years ago. My belief is that the two can work together and support each other. The story remains the star and the most important thing. **I believe that strong media relationships are as vital in a business as an email list.** And in this book, my main focus is to speak to you as a journalist who sits in a newsroom. I'm going to tell you how best to communicate with this person.

When working in the media, I inhabited a sometimes crazy and unpredictable world on a daily basis. One minute it was full of excitement or shock due to a major election surprise, a gun attack or a celebrity visit. The next, I was reporting from an inquest and listening to evidence about the third suicide on that day's case list. Other days and certain times of the year, I'd find myself sitting there scratching my head wondering if someone will send in something that I can turn into a good story. Or I was ringing contacts looking for follow-ups or asking for comments on a story I was trying to develop or a feature piece that I'd been working on for months. There are times of the year and every journalist is aware of them, that are much quieter than others and that is when journalists need to do a lot more work to get stories. And if you are ready to go with your story at any of those times, you have already massively increased your chances of getting featured.

There were times as a journalist when certain stories grabbed me and there were others that required a lot more effort to get but both were worth it. **If there is a story there, good, or bad, a good journalist will go to any lengths to get it.** I know this because I went to great lengths to get stories ahead of my competitors. Having said all this, some of the best stories I've written featured ordinary people who had lives worthy of a film. These are the people I always think of when I see a seemingly ordinary person making international headlines for something they have achieved.

Try to look at media publications in their paper format - at least once

When I think of journalism, I always think first of how stories look on a physical page. This to me is still hugely important despite the advent of online outlets and social media. As a starting point, it is good to look at stories on the physical page as it is a good way to get more familiar with what is inside and the opportunities that are there. It can be difficult to see opportunities on a webpage and especially when you can get distracted more easily by stories that are promoted on the page and by pop-up adverts trying to get your attention.

Whereas, on a physical page, you look at one page at a time and you get a better insight into what goes where and what journalist does what. You can also do this by getting a pdf copy of an issue and looking at it on screen. But me being old school, I like to circle stories, columns, opinions pieces – all of which are important to know about when you need to pitch a story to that outlet. I recommend that you do this during your early days of research (at least once) as this will stand to you hugely in the months and years ahead.

This also feeds into how you can find other ways to get featured outside of a press release. And I have a list of ideas that will help you think about your story differently and to think outside of the usual routes to get publicity.

A journey worth taking

This book will give you an insight into how the media works, the inner workings of a newsroom, and how you can get more coverage by understanding what journalists want. Getting featured is about learning how to link your needs with the needs of a journalist who wants to tell newsworthy stories to their readers, listeners, and viewers.

Getting publicity is not instant. Yes, major publicity can happen fast, but this is not the norm. It requires work, hard graft and a willingness to wait for the right moment to pitch (I know this can be really hard). It is also about building relationships, something few people spend time doing. They want publicity fast, but they don't realize that journalists need to get to know you, your story and how they can fit it into their story list.

Remember, a journalist has to pitch your story to an editor once they sift through all their emails and find a gem of a story that they want to write. Oftentimes, an editor will want the journalist to pitch the story again in another news meeting with a different angle. So, it's about a journey. The journey you take and the journey your story takes once a journalist wants to cover it. It's a much longer journey if you are planning to feature in major outlets, but not as long if you are happy to stay local. The latter, in my opinion, can be the best decision for some. I know many companies big and small that have good relationships with local media, and this is all they concentrate on, and they get great results. They also support this with their online efforts. Working with a local journalist is a guaranteed learning experience. If you put the time and effort into your journey in local and trade outlets, you will reap huge benefits from building lasting connections that will bring rewards time and time again.

It involves some hard graft, a lot of thinking about how you can make your business newsworthy and keep it newsworthy. It involves knowing what you want to share, what a journalist wants you to share, and ultimately what you are happy with sharing. For many, the journey is a difficult, frustrating, and an energy-sapping process. This is why determination and encouragement are essential. I want to encourage you to take the steps to getting media publicity. Throughout this book, I have placed some mantras and tools to help you. **Information is great, but emotion is important, too. This is important when embarking on building media relationships.**

Media Mantra

I know that mindset and confidence issues can raise their heads at any time during this journey. This is why I would like to share some motivational tips to help you get started and keep going. Read this mantra and then fill in your answers.

Mantra: To get media publicity, I will find my story because I love my business enough to want to tell it.

Please do each of the following to get you started in a confident way:

1. Make a list of 3 or more reasons why you deserve publicity

2. What was the last story you read/saw/listened to that interested you and that made you think about getting featured in the media?

3. What is one great thing that you could make happen if you started to get featured in the media and built a profile?

CHAPTER 2

GETTING TO THE STARTING BLOCKS

Do you remember when you got your first car? Okay, stick with me here. My first car was a 1990 blue Nissan Micra, and I loved that car so much. The number plate had my birthday on it, so it was extra special and I saw it as my lucky charm. I went on lots of small journeys, to the shopping centre and back, to the park and back, to the beach and back. But I wanted more from it. I wanted to go further but didn't have the courage. Longer journeys took courage, especially driving for the first time by myself. When I did venture further away from my smaller trips, it felt amazing. It was on these trips that I learned more about my driving and the area around me.

Media relations is a lot like this. You seek it out in short-term ways when you want some attention for a new project, a new employee, a launch, or a major achievement you or your company has achieved. This publicity is satisfying, for sure, but it can be short-lived, and the attention and buzz you receive is quickly forgotten. Sometimes, these short bursts of media activity can be enough, but to keep your business in the public's mind, you need to

build in more consistency into your media publicity strategy.
You also need to know **WHY** you want to do this
What are your goals for doing this?
Is this the best option for you at this time?
Are you ready? (See my checklist at the end of this book to help you decide).

Let me break this down a little for you:

Personal Goals: Are you ready to put yourself forward as an expert and show more of yourself to the world?

Business Goals: Are you looking to sell tickets to an event? Increase email sign-ups? Write guest posts?

Team Goals: Do you want to build creativity within your organisation, so you can get more attention via online channels and through media outlets?

Revenue Goals: Do you want/need to increase revenue and need more warm leads coming to your business?

Budget: Having a budget or at least some funding put aside to help you in your PR efforts is a good idea if you can afford it. Yes, you will get the media coverage for free but think about the time and resources you will need to have in place to achieve this. You may need to hire someone to do research if you don't have time to do it yourself, to track pitches and follow-ups, to connect with journalists on Twitter and elsewhere. If you feel you cannot give this activity sufficient time in your weekly schedule, then I suggest you look for someone who can give you 2-3 hours per week to provide information to you so you can then act on it. Many entrepreneurs manage to do this themselves to start with because they have no budget. If you can get someone on your team or an outsider to help you with some of this, it will help you to concentrate more on your message and put together a strategy based on this information.

Also, to build on your PR efforts and to continue to spread your message, having a budget for advertising is an added bonus but not essential (note: some media outlets will ask about your advertising budget upfront so be prepared for that and decide what you want to do. I deal more with this in the chapter on Supplements).

With an overarching WHY, you can then proceed more clearly with how you want to do things instead of writing a press release and sending it to everyone and anyone who might be interested.

What you really need is a longer-term impact and a desire to build relationships with journalists, so that they end up contacting you, not the other way around. You want to take the longer journey whether that is in a Micra or an Audi is up you! However, many find that making this step can be difficult to get right, as building relationships takes time, skill, and the ability to know when to pitch and what to pitch in order to keep you newsworthy without being overexposed. Maybe you've had one or two pieces in the paper, and that's it. Or maybe you haven't gotten a reply to any of your pitches. This can be devastating, but many people start there and break through only after staying consistent, persevering and both learning and refining their message, so they get to know how the media game works.

You need to adapt your message to suit and to be comfortable with adapting it enough to grab a journalist's attention. You may need to adapt it several times and this is okay. Many PR professionals do this all the time. **And journalists are used to getting stories pitched to them in different ways with a different angle. Oftentimes, they don't have time to think of a better angle and that is where you come in with the help that they need to see your story in a different light.** No matter what stage you are at, everyone, at some point, wants to build long-term relationships. But this isn't possible unless you're in this for the long haul. Building your credibility and confidence takes time. Just like learning to drive!

Some ways to get you thinking about this

Be reliable

If you are at the start and have never pitched a story to a journalist, you should keep this in mind and be reliable from the offset. If a journalist asks you to get back with new quotes from your spokesperson, you get them over that day or the next day. **Always ask for a deadline and meet it.** If a journalist needs you to clarify something, you should be able to do it right there and then or ask someone to check it immediately. If you say you are going to do something, do it.

Even more importantly, if you can't do it or if you know that the request will take time to get, **be honest and upfront**. Don't be the person who says yes to impossible tasks. It could take days for your CEO to give you quotes and for these quotes to be cleared by management. As a sole business owner, you may be juggling a lot of things at once and you will need time to rethink your quotes or to clarify something. A journalist is aware of this, but he/she may be willing to wait if those quotes are vital to the story. Just keep them up to date on what is happening. Don't go cold and work on getting the quotes alone. Let them know when they will be sent over and if you manage to get it done quicker, then bonus points for you!

Look at your story from other points of view beyond your own

Think about readers and journalists. These two are intricately linked. A journalist is always thinking of readers/listeners/viewers – their audience, some of which are paying a monthly subscription for their service. If you are seen as a reliable and knowledgeable source to a journalist, you will automatically represent the same in their mind to readers and viewers. **Don't always think of your story as something you are doing or launching.** Think of what you are doing and how it helps to shine a light on an issue, a solution, an area, or a person. Landing a story in the media can happen in the most unusual ways. And it's not always the obvious that lands the coverage. The less obvious stories often get the most attention (hence you should seek angles outside of yourself).

Examples: I worked closely for many years with a host of different photographers, however this time it was different. This photographer put himself in the limelight and reignited his career by publishing photos of his feet, accompanied by written journal accounts while on a foot detox treatment. His openness and honesty attracted readers and people became familiar with his work and slowly the interest grew. He showed vulnerability, talked about his own life and the issues he faced. The toxins leaving his body through his feet showed that he needed to take care of himself more, and he started to do that, as well as encouraging his social media followers to do the same. His route to publicity was through his own personal health journey.

I have written about a boxer who turned his hand to cooking and was asked to write a column about healthy eating for a magazine. He went on to publish a range of articles and decided to go back to college to study nutrition, in particular for boxers.

I have also written about a qualified lawyer turned fashion lover who landed her dream job writing a social column and commenting on social events. Her email would flood with requests from people who wanted her to cover their event. This was a side job for her, but it got her loads of publicity as the "lawyer by day, social columnist by night". She would get her photo taken with any celebrities that were there, get some quotes from attendees and all this helped boost her profile.

These people show that it is not the typical that gets the best results. Journalists see that all the time. The three people I mentioned above should have been getting media coverage for doing what they were qualified to do: take photos, win boxing matches, and defend people in court. I give these examples to show you **how you need to think widely about how to get coverage and be willing to angle your story in such a way as to fit a certain topic or theme.** If you have an interesting hobby, an employee doing amazing charity work, a collaboration with another business coming up, look at these for angles.

Don't settle for the obvious route. Journalists get these all day, every day. You'll stand out if you avoid the obvious. When you are next looking for publicity, ask yourself: could I get someone from a different area of expertise to be my spokesperson? Choose someone people wouldn't expect, and you'll automatically stand out that bit more. This can add a different flavour to your content. A boxer doing a healthy eating column is one such example.

Surprising a journalist is difficult, but trying hard will get you noticed

I once received a fruit hamper every week for a month from a juice company. A plant was delivered to my workplace every day for a week from a dating agency (They knew I preferred plants to flowers). I could go on. I'm not trying to encourage sending gifts to journalists, by the way. While this type of media relations can be memorable, don't go down this route unless it is warranted and fits into your campaign and messaging. Some journalists don't like to get gifts so be aware of this. In fact, some journalists really detest this and see it as irrelevant (there are exceptions like beauty journalists who need to see and test the product). Remember that gifts don't make stories. They can only act to amplify your message.

Don't send journalists something that doesn't directly link to the reason why you are doing it. Don't send a promotional t-shirt from a past campaign because it would be a nice idea. Be intentional. You will see beauty companies be very intentional about this. Always ask yourself what is it doing to further your business? Have an end goal in mind and build momentum by being consistent in what you send and the message that goes along with it. The two should be linked.

You could send, for example, one product a week from an eco-friendly range to a national beauty journalist. Each product complements the previous one and when the journalist receives all of them, he/she knows that you are building out a new range that delivers a new result for customers. At this point, you could arrange for the journalist to take a class (online or in person) in applying the products or you could invite the journalist to meet the team making the products. Hosting a live video training series which could be shared on the media outlet's platform is also an option. If the journalist is excited about the product, he/she may agree to do a live training with you on one of the social media channels. When doing any of this activity, always have a call to action that serves readers and in turns serves you. Alternatively, you could offer a valuable giveaway to readers. Also include a trial of the products, so they know exactly what they do, and they will rave about them to their family, friends and online.

To go back to the fruit hamper company and the dating agency that I mentioned earlier. I eventually wrote stories about both of these businesses, but they weren't directly about either of them. Reminder: journalists don't write advertorials dressed up as news stories (more on what I mean by that later). They do get asked to write advertorial copy, but it is labelled as such and the content is written accordingly.

Articles were written when they were ready for the audience

I wrote these stories but only when the timing was right for me to do a piece that had value and that was newsworthy to readers. One of the stories was about the best fruit and vegetables to include in a juice drink to help fight cancer which was backed up with recent evidence, and an interview with a reputable cancer spokesperson that I knew from previous coverage. The story had more weight because of the inclusion of the expert. In dealing with something serious like cancer, a journalist will want to do their research and offer an article of value.

The other article was about giving separated men advice on finding love again. The latter involved interviewing a relationship expert, and I included only a couple of relevant quotes from the dating agency. Despite the stories not being directly about either of the businesses, both of them got great publicity because they were part of a news story that had value. In fact, I would argue that their publicity efforts received a huge boost because of the work put in by the journalist to write a story that was directly speaking to readers. Both businesses had a feature news piece that they could use to further their publicity and to show to stakeholders or future investors.

This shows you that when you pitch, you may not get featured straight away or even in a few weeks or months. The journalist may receive your email and mark it for a future feature idea or supplement that is happening weeks or months from now. A journalist also needs time to work on it and to delve deeper into the subject to provide a more rounded and high value piece. Which in the end is good for readers and in turn good for you as the piece will come across as a strong and professionally researched article that will get attention from other experts in the field. It will also be a lot more engaging to the audience and once published to other media outlets who may like to do their own piece on it.

The difference between a story and an advertorial

I think it is important at this point to differentiate between a story and an advertorial. I want to do this early in this book because I feel it is such an important distinguishing factor into having a salesy story versus having a news story. When you send in your press release, journalists can instantly tell whether there is a story there or if it is an advertorial for your business. You may not think it, but readers can often tell the difference too.

Advertorial: This is an advertisement article giving information about a product or service from the seller's point of view (you get to review it and decide on how big you want the piece to be depending on your budget). Normally, it is in the style of an editorial piece that highlights elements of the product or service. It almost always includes testimonials and a consumer photo. You will have noticed these in publications, although nowadays they are more inclined to fit in with the rest of the content in a publication as opposed to sticking out as much as they used to in the past. However, advertorials need to be labelled as such and you'll often see words like "paid for promotion" or "promotion" on these pieces. Audiences are obliged to know that you paid for it, much like how online influencers need to be transparent and tell you that they are getting paid for a post.

What I often found during my time in newsrooms is that I would get advertorial style pieces dressed as press releases and it was my job to turn them into a news story. Which isn't impossible but you are asking the journalist to do all the work. Turning an advertorial into a news story requires going back to the start and finding that story's place in the news agenda. You have possibly provided a good starting point if your content is presented in an easy to read and digestible way but the journalist reading it will have to try to connect it to the wider news cycle by coming up with ideas to make it a news story. That is really your job. You should be providing the ideas for a news story and beginning the conversation with the journalist about its news value. If you want your advertorial to run as is, then you are better off considering paying for an advertising space.

News story: This is a story that has its context rooted in the news of the day. It is written by a journalist based on their own initiative or it could be something sent into them either in a pitch email or press release or it could be a follow-up to a previous story he/she wrote. It informs the public in an objective way and its aim is to get two sides of the story if this is deemed necessary. A story is full of facts, professionally researched, and can be either a soft or hard story, depending on the angle taken.

Stories and advertorials both have their place in media outlets. Both serve a purpose. And both can do their jobs very well. Nowadays, many advertorials seek to appeal more to readers by being less salesy and less obvious, but if it is an advertorial, it must be presented as one to the reader or viewer. Savvy readers will identify them even without the label. They won't be fooled.

Imagine that I wrote advertorials about both of the businesses mentioned above. I took their press releases and turned them into advertorial pieces based entirely on what they had sent me. Readers would get the information, and those interested would read or at least skim the piece, but they wouldn't be emotionally invested in the story. And those with no interest in either subject would go straight past these advertorials.

When it is written as a news story or a feature that is researched, respects the reader, and appeals to human emotions, you have a better chance that readers will stop to read it. They are drawn to it because it tells a story and doesn't have that feeling of an advertorial, an advert dressed as a story. That said, advertorials still present a valuable opportunity to tell your story your way. That is, of course, if you have the budget to do so.

Your angle

You've probably heard this many times. What's the angle? In terms of media publicity, the angle is your way in, your way of grabbing that first initial interest of the journalist you sent your story pitch to. Every story needs an angle, a point of interest, something that touches people. If a pitch is overly salesy, any decent journalist will look at it and ask, "Where is the story here? What can I do with this?" And that is when they may, at best, give a short amount of his/her pressurised time in the newsroom to consider news angles based on your piece. They just as easily might not. And just like that, your story pitch gets binned. This is why you should **offer a story, not a sales pitch.** I hear you; this can be hard to do, especially if you are new to this.

So, this is my biggest tip: **Make it about the reader** and how your story helps them do something useful, prevents them from making a mistake or informs them of something coming in the future, for example, a new product or service, a trend in your area or something you feel should be adopted by government or a government agency. Make the reader, i.e., your target audience member, the star of your pitch or press release and you stand a much greater chance of getting featured. Take you and your company out of the leading role and put the reader/listener in there instead. You will quickly find that you are writing a completely different story pitch, one that has an element of news to it, one that will interest a journalist. All a journalist cares about is their audience. Speak to them and you've got the journalist's attention. Speak to them and you will start to see interest in your business grow and new clients knocking at your door.

How do I know if I have a story to tell?

Not everything you've ever done or are going to do in your business is a story. Let's get that straight first. It is about knowing when it is and how to write it, so it lands on a reporter's desk as a story they want to write. My first piece of advice is to step back from your product/service/business and ask yourself why you started it in the first place.

These are specific questions I encourage you to ask yourself about your business idea:

- Did it come from a personal experience you had?
- Or a business experience you had with another company?
- Did it come from a time when you were unemployed?
- Did you hate your job and want to give yourself another option?
- Did you read an article which sowed the seed of your business idea? (Having the article to use in your pitch or as an attachment to your press release would be great).
- Where were you when it happened?
- At home? While walking in a local beauty spot, observing something in a nearby park?
- Or did it come to you when you were on holiday, sitting on a sun lounger?
- Were you talking to a friend who had always wanted to start a business and work for themselves? They never did it, but always wished they had tried. You thought you could do it and maybe you now want to share some of your success with them.

"Think Week"

To find answers and inspiration, I urge you to sit down in your most comfortable place – the couch, your garden, a park bench near your house, wherever – go there and think it out. Even better, if you can, do what Microsoft founder Bill Gates does and go for a "Think Week", where you can be in a quiet space, away from distractions and just allow your mind the space to think. A "Think Week" might be unrealistic for you time wise but maybe try a "Think Day" or a "Think Hour". Doing this will serve you well in thinking out your goals and, from a media point of view, your potential stories. You may decide that you have a story with multiple strands, and you want to plan it out over a year's worth of content. Or maybe you want to offer an exclusive interview about a time in your life. Doing this allows you to focus solely on creating story ideas that you can further flesh out when you get back to the desk or when you share them with your team.

Ask yourself the questions listed above. This is where your journey towards getting media attention should start. But remember, it's only a start. The answers to these questions will sow the seed of a story generation process, one that involves other people, whether positive or negative, your inspiration to start your business, the problem you wanted to solve, and any problems you had along the way. It all stems from here. Then, the work starts in putting the stories together.

Story Boxes

This is where I ask you to put your story ideas into distinct boxes with different labels on. I ask you to do this because each story deserves some kind of lens in which to see it through as a starting point. Doing this makes it easier to see where the story angle is.

These are my four distinct story boxes:

Transformational: How did you go from point A in your business/life to point B? This is the before and after type story that remains a hugely popular way of telling any type of story. You will most likely have read many of these.

Quick-Growth: This is when you applied a new technique or upgraded an old one and your business grew exponentially overnight. The tactics and tools you used to grow your business and make it successful.

Turnaround: This is where you brought your business back from the brink. Where you thought you couldn't do it, the sacrifices you made, the hurdles you had to jump to make it work.

Discovery: You figured out something and you want to share it with others. This discovery can make a huge difference in the lives of others, it can save them time, money, and years of not knowing how to solve this particular problem.

Ask yourself: What was the catalyst that made me choose what I did? This doesn't have to be a major thing. It can be something as small as reading an inspirational quote online posted by someone you admire in your area of business. Think of the stories you can offer instead of thinking of media publicity as something you do only when you need to. This is a major mindset change but is one that will open up so many more avenues to publicity because you will be cultivating story ideas consistently not just when you need to. This will further help your chances of building relationships with journalists and editors. They will get to know you as someone who provides value to your area of expertise consistently and not just at the times when you need to get featured. Now, let me tell you about how a novelty cake business started my journey into the world of media.

CHAPTER 3

THE CAKE THAT MADE THE HEADLINES

My first published news story was about a bakery in my hometown outside Galway, in the west of Ireland. It was the first bakery to open in the town for many years. Nothing majorly exciting there, but I sensed there was a story there that might be worth telling, if I dug deep enough. The bakery specialised in novelty cakes in the shape of bridges, castles, scenes from around Ireland…you get the picture. But this was Ireland in the 1990s, and novelty cakes were still... well a novelty. I hadn't seen a bakery with these kinds of cakes before, and I felt there could be an interesting story here.

I was a keen freelancer at the time, just starting out. I was looking to get a place on a prestigious Master's university course in journalism, and I needed to get three stories published as part of my application. As I walked around my hometown, something instinctively told me to go in and check out this new business. I asked the owners some questions and after if they would be interested in me telling their story so I could write it for a local newspaper. I'd do the research, interview them, and observe them for a day. Within the first few minutes of meeting them, I knew they had a great story to tell. The cakes were pretty amazing to look at, never mind eat! Of course, they were also photogenic, and journalism, despite being so synonymous with words, is heavily reliant on images.

I pitched a scenario to them. We could get word out through the local newsletter, put up some posters and decorate the front of their shop to invite locals to try cake on a certain date and time. This would coincide with an invitation for a press photographer to come by and take some photos. I would organise the date with the photographer first and, in the meantime, I would write and pitch their story to the newspaper's editor. I was just starting off and didn't know how this was going to go but I had that intuitive feeling that there was something here worth pursuing. **I encourage you to listen to your intuition and what it is trying to tell you when you are pitching stories out to the media.**

They were flabbergasted and couldn't believe their story would be of any interest to anyone. They were nervous about contacting the media and were worried about negative publicity or if something inaccurate was said about them. It seemed that they were confident that, in time, people would get to know they were open, and that would be enough. They were happy to wait months, even years, to see a steady flow of customers. "But an article in the local newspaper would get your message out to so many people," I told them. I waited for a couple of days, then popped in again. I knew it was going to be tough to convince them.

Between the first and second meetings, I had written down a list of ideas about their business, the angles we could take, and which outlets I would send the story to. The latter was of particular interest to them, as they had never dealt with a journalist before. I was interested to tell their story, and from my knowledge of the local papers, I knew where it could fit. I observed them for a day, chatted with their customers, interviewed both owners during their breaks and, of course, ate a lot of cake. I said to myself, "You know this could be where you start your career if you get this story right. It could get you your place on this course and set you off on the way to becoming a journalist." I was excited, for myself and for the owners of the bakery. **Don't forget, journalists are ambitious, too.** And remember, they all start somewhere and know (but do forget) how hard it is to get your foot in the door.

The cake was tasty!

I wrote the story, and I was excited about seeing it in print. But the work was only starting. I had to pitch it. My pitch to the newspaper focused on several things, but basically, I told them the focus would be on these two women who had lost their jobs and met in the unemployment queue, then decided to have a coffee. That coffee spawned a business idea, and they learned how to make these novelty cakes that people had only ever associated with America. They invested hundreds of hours working on their baking skills in their kitchens at home, meeting up at weekends to discuss what worked and what didn't. I had some photos of them in their kitchens which for one publication was their main focus. They were interested in seeing the very beginnings of the business and the struggles of the time just added to the intrigue (they actually went on to do a series on the early days of start-ups). In the piece, I used some quotes from the women about their sacrifices in the early days and what it was like starting a business as a woman in Ireland in the late 90s (supports were not like they are now).

I took pictures of the women, the cakes, and a few with customers, just by way of having visuals. They were certainly not good enough print quality. I sent in a short pitch and a press release, some photos, then waited. Two days later, I got a call from an editor, who asked some questions and said he would like to do a two-page feature. I was overjoyed. Feature pieces need a lot of space in a newspaper, so I knew the story would get a lot of attention. The editor said he'd send their press photographer and asked if I could set a suitable time to get some photos taken (we already had one in mind!). We put our plan into action, and we were lucky our timing worked. We were getting the word out in the newsletter, and we put out a simple poster board that read "Try some free pieces of a castle chocolate cake at x day at x time".

The press photoshoot

It isn't easy to excite a seasoned press photographer. However, when he saw the crowd, the cakes and the excitement, his energy was high, and his excitement transferred across to everyone. He got a ladder from a hardware shop down the street and took an aerial shot of the customers and shop owners outside the bakery. This all felt like a dream to the two women business owners, but it also showed them the power of media publicity first-hand. And the power of rallying your community around you (essentially, your email list these days).

The article appeared with some changes to what I had submitted. This was my first experience of this, but as I know now, this happens all the time. I wasn't annoyed by it; it made my piece much better. Journalists and editors change content to suit the story they want to tell their audience. It is good for you to hear this now rather than later when the journalist decides to take a totally different angle to the one you thought was the story. The two women were beyond thrilled at the coverage and the goodwill that they had generated in the space of just three weeks since my arrival at their shop to the publication of the article.

Why it is best to start local

Media begets media, but how are you going to get media if you pitch to national outlets and your pitch gets lost in the middle of hundreds of others? You will get noticed more often and quicker if you have already received publicity. The best place to start getting featured is locally.

When my story about the bakery appeared in print, it went across two pages in the main section of the newspaper. The bakery owners were thrilled, and they saw results instantly after it was published. They couldn't believe it. People came into the shop to congratulate them, and they started to see a major upsurge in customers and orders for novelty cakes. I went to visit them shortly afterwards, and I encouraged them to cut out the article and frame it on the wall for people to see rather than keeping it neatly folded away in a drawer (this was sharing back then! There was no social media). When they put it on their wall, it became a talking point among customers. Conversations reminded them of how important it was to nurture and build relationships with local media. They were about to realise just how important it was as their media presence started to grow.

The publicity they received as a result of the local piece led to local radio interviews, a magazine shoot, and an interview in a round-up of quirky stories broadcast by a national radio station. Much later, one of the owners was interviewed on national television as part of a "Cakes for Christmas" feature. All of this came from this first piece I wrote, but ultimately from their story, which had huge potential. It was a story they thought no one would be interested in. I knew that a large feature would get the attention of other journalists both local and national. They had a strong visual story, one that would come across well on television. I never guarantee that this will happen, but sometimes you just have a feeling, you just know it will take off and one article begets the next one.

The best thing that came from it all was that it gave them the confidence and knowledge to take it further without my help. They were more comfortable about being interviewed and felt confident enough to phone newspapers, and tell them what they were planning, asking if they might be interested in doing a story.

The one thing I always felt about them was they were never pushy. If the media outlet wasn't interested, they wouldn't give up, but they wouldn't push the same story again and again. They would find a new angle. And they certainly wouldn't keep ringing the office to ask why the newspaper wouldn't cover it. They would try to understand why the story wasn't picked up, then come up with something different and better next time they went to pitch. The main piece of advice you can take from this is: **be positive and persistent, but never pushy**.

Front page image

Three weeks before Valentine's Day, they were the ones that called that same local paper that published their first story and said they were making this special cake for a party for Valentine's Day for a couple who were celebrating 60 years of marriage. The newspaper editor jumped at the opportunity, and the cake featured on the front page of that week's issue. A front-page image is a life-changing event for a business. They realised this after the reaction they received, seeing how it snowballed, how it was followed by requests for radio interviews, with more articles and magazines seeking them for features. They got more coverage on television, and my mother began phoning me to tell me about the latest time she saw them in the paper or on the radio or television. I was so happy seeing how they'd dared to build on what I had helped them start.

Be courageous

There are three main things to take away from this. Firstly, **don't be afraid to talk about your business in a more personal way**, to talk about yourself, not just your business. Secondly, **be proactive about building on your publicity** by instigating an interesting photo opportunity, suggesting an idea for a press release, or pitching a story idea to a radio or television station. Lastly, **focus first on local media**, as this ultimately gives you the best chance to get featured. Local media is a major focal point for national journalists looking for stories. Locals looks to nationals for stories and vice versa. Local journalists pitch stories they've already written to national publications if they feel it should have a wider audience. During my time as a journalist, local and national journalists helped each other out especially when a major story broke, and it made sense to work together.

Look, I'm not saying that everything you've ever done in your life or business is newsworthy. What I hope this story does though is encourage you to look at things differently. By pitching your story with a different mindset and with a more personality-driven tone, along with understanding how the media works, and how journalists think, you will start to see results. It will have a wider impact on your business and will generate positive energy, and a feeling of fulfilment for you and your colleagues.

CHAPTER 4

THE ROUTES YOU CAN TAKE

There are many ways you can seek media publicity outside of sending a press release. Here, I go through some approaches which will help you decide what other ways can work best for you. A press release is not the only way although I have included it here as it remains the most popular and many journalists still want to receive them. But others hate them and want to read a short pitch in an email that helps them decide if they want to go after your story. You need to know which one suits your story best. I'm going to show the most common ways to seek publicity and then ways you may never have thought of.

PRESS RELEASE: This is where you map out your story from start to finish, choosing one angle, one headline, one sub-headline, a photo, and quotes, and adding your contact details at the end. **You start your press release with the most pertinent details. Forget what you were taught in school about leaving the interesting part at the end.** Turn this idea upside down and put the most interesting, often the most up-to-date aspect at the very top, then work backwards to detail how the story transpired. Yes, this requires a total mind shift, but if you start at the origins of your story and expect a journalist to read to the end to get to the pertinent detail, then you have no chance.

The pertinent detail

To give a simple example, take these three first paragraphs. Which one should come first in a press release?

1. Never did Molly Baker ever think that in her 20 years of business, that she would have made cakes for every celebrity that ever visited the town.

2. Foxtown's popular bakery Molly's Cakes opens this week after surviving an arson attack that almost destroyed the business.

3. Arson attacks are up 20 percent nationwide from this time last year, yet a celebrity baker is determined to not be just another statistic and is back behind the counter.

Did you pick one? Let's look at them in more detail.

Number 1 - This one isn't a bad angle to pursue, and it could be a good starting point to a large feature piece that gives an in-depth view of Molly's career. But as a news story, this would not be the best angle to start with.

Number 2 - Look at the second one, this has a pertinent detail - the arson attack and this is vital to get into the first paragraph. This gives weight to the story and draws the reader into the story instantly. Readers want to know what happened next. And those that didn't know about the arson attack will be drawn in to catch up on what they missed.

Number 3 - Now look at the third one. It doesn't have Molly's name but focuses in on a national statistic. This is a national newspaper following up on a local story but nationalising it for readers by putting a wider scope on the piece and grabbing the attention by using the latest statistics on arson attacks. They then go on to humanise the statistics by using Molly's story as an example. Thereby, putting a personal perspective on what these statistics mean to ordinary people. Each of these paragraphs serve a purpose. However, the pertinent detail is the arson attack and the owner's determination to not let it close her business. For a news story, this is vital to have up front. The other details that are needed at the start are the name of the shop and when it is reopening. Along with the fact that the business was almost destroyed, these are all pertinent details too but not as important as the mention of the arson attack.

Press releases can be sent to any type of media outlet but note that some outlets like to receive what is called a media pitch email. This is where all the details are in the body of the email with any extra supporting information linked to within the email. There are no attachments. I go into more detail on press releases and pitch emails in future chapters. Below, I want to give you an insight into what I mean when I say a pitch email.

PITCH EMAIL: I will focus more on writing these later in the book but for some journalists, this is the optimal way to get their attention. In essence, **a pitch email is a shorter version of a press release and is written in the body of an email**. A pitch will suit journalists who have tighter deadlines. I recommend that you keep the word count be between 200- 300 words maximum. The shorter, the better. These are ideal for television reporters, as they can tell instantly whether the story is worth pursuing. They don't have the time or the interest to read a press release. Tell them in a few sentences what your story is, and your chances of getting a response have already skyrocketed.

There are no attachments; all you need to say is placed in the body of the email. In fact, I don't recommend attachments at all unless the journalist asks for a file to be sent. Link out to your website, social media, and any files you need the journalist to look at. Your pitch should link in with something that is happening right now or something that is about to happen or has happened but is still newsworthy. Think timeliness when pitching to television reporters and researchers. Email pitches work well for national and international news journalists who get so many emails that it is a relief to open an email that has a short pitch inside. If it is a story that they want to do, they will call you or email back (most likely call if time is tight) as their deadlines run much regularly than regional or local journalists. So, you need to be ready to respond **right then and there**. Be ready to take their call. Be by your email if you pitch a story to these people. If they ring and you don't pick up, they will move on to the next story. Television reporting is especially fast paced, so keep this in mind. Don't take that Buddhist temple retreat the week that you send in your pitch!

PHOTO: A good photo with a good caption is usually enough to achieve substantial publicity. A photo used well in a newspaper will get you much more attention than a 500-word press release buried somewhere in the middle or back sections. Think imagery as well as content. When you go down this route and many choose this one alone, you need to be able to tell your story through the photo. Always remember the wise words of Ansel Adams, "You don't take a photo, you make it." Put time and consideration into how you make your photo. This is a particular skill, and you should hire a photographer with press experience to work with you to achieve this. The experience a photographer will bring will be invaluable to achieving publicity for your photo idea.

When a journalist receives a good photo, they will automatically think of where it can be used. Sometimes he/she might decide to get more of the story but if the photo is telling the story, then there won't be a need to do this. When you pitch your photo for publicity purposes, don't be tempted to give a huge story with it. If you are using images as your main method of publicity, then, let the photo do the talking. Trust that all you need is a good caption to go with something that is eye-catching, entertaining, or educational and put a call to action in there like your website or a date for an event if the photo is promoting one. Something that gets eyes on your business. Captions should never run over 100 – 120 words. 150 words is okay if required to give all the pertinent information that the photo needs.

PHOTO ESSAY: A photo essay is a series of images that reveal a story about a person or a subject. They tend to evoke emotion, be thought-provoking, highlight an issue that unsettles the reader or go behind the scenes of someone's life or work. They can be funny too. This is a publicity route that is largely underutilized by businesses who opt for the regular single photo, but I encourage you to think about this as a way of pitching your story in a different way. If you set up your pitch in an interesting way, telling the journalist how many photos you think you have, the story behind the images and why you think it is worthy of a photo essay, then you can work with him/her in setting up a shoot with one of their photographers. Or, if you have a relationship with a good photographer, you can work on this together and then pitch it. Your pitch to the journalists should highlight your collaboration, the types of photos and the location. You should pitch it before any photo is taken. This way you will get some vital insights from the journalist as to what he/she thinks might work well.

The photo essay is a wonderful form of visual storytelling that isn't seen that often in the media and is one that isn't pitched that often either. It is often photographers that have this idea when they go to photograph a person or a scene or an issue. It is then that the photographer realizes that in order to tell the full story he/she is going to need more than one photo. And that is when a photo essay works really well.

When you hire your own photographer or the news outlet sends out their photographer, make sure you are ready to spend quality time on the project. Your series of photos need to tell your story piece by piece. They need to progress the story. Surprising the viewer is key also. One which may suit businesses more is a day-in-the-life type of photo essay. Another idea is to take the images in a completely different surrounding than you are normally in. An historical setting near you could be worth looking at as a location. Remember though you will have to think of the photos as mini stories told visually. You will need 10 strong images that make the final selection so you may need to have hundreds taken to start with. But you will quickly realize what works and what narrative you are trying to tell. All 10 won't get used but to tell a photo essay in an engaging way, the minimum that I have seen working well is 5 that are picked from a possible 10. Remember that photo essays will require a lot of time in planning, preparing those being photographed and editing. Also, don't lose sight that the photo essay needs to reveal something; it needs to draw in the viewer. If you are new to using photos as a way of getting publicity, this would not be an option I would recommend early on. Get more familiar with what works by homing in on getting good single-use media photos first.

LETTER TO THE EDITOR: Letters to the editor are still widely read and a popular go-to section for readers who want to get reaction to the big stories happening at the time. They are read more regularly around major times like elections, sports events or when a celebrity does something that transcends the celeb pages. This is a route that is not taken by many but if you can position yourself correctly and write a letter that is relevant, timely and in response to a recent happening, you will get an editor's attention.

Remember that there is a technique to writing letters to the editor. Get familiar with the letters page that you are planning to send to as a starting point. You can write a letter explaining what side you are on regarding a certain issue, your thoughts on a particular story you read in the newspaper you are sending or offer a new way of looking at an old issue. Letter writing is a skill, and I don't encourage you to solely focus on this. Before trying this as a method of publicity, I encourage you to read the letters pages numerous times and around the times of major events. This way, you will start to see what types of letters get published. You will also start to see how people position themselves as experts when writing letters.

Having said all of this, this is an option that is vastly underutilised, but is one you should consider, especially when you want to make a point about an issue, and you feel you have the expertise to speak about it. Be sure that you write it with your expert hat on and don't use it as a way to advertise anything. Letters are not for advertising your business or product. Neither are they a vehicle for dressing up a press release and putting it in letter format. Once your letter is accepted, you will get the chance to see what edits are being made and what job/title you want to be used with your name. Make sure this title is something you can be found for relatively easily online as people will search for information about you once they read your letter. Do some research into the words used widely in the area that your letter will focus on. Some keyword research is a good idea but remember not to stuff them all into it. Your letter will not get considered if you do this. Write your letter with the reader in mind first and foremost.

Just make sure you don't ruminate on your letter for too long. Timing is everything when it comes to letter writing. Make sure your letter is timely and has something significant to say. This is a competitive section, and your writing needs to be punchy, straightforward, and newsy. It is a time-dependent section and is limited on space too.

VIDEO: Can you tell your news story on video? Can you get a customer to appear in it? Can you do a short interview with a customer? If you do this well and present it like a news segment, a media outlet may use it on their website, and it could well get publicity on TV shows, too. They may even do a news story on it, especially if your video is popular, funny, timely, well-researched and presented well. If it is possible, try to bring some humour into the video, by way of an introduction or some music or an interesting outro. Draw in the viewer, in this case, the journalist, by standing out a little more in how you present the video.

Take a look at how some influencers on Instagram do their showreels and take some inspiration from them regarding using music, props, outdoor or indoor settings and how to do product placement in an interesting way. On video, it is important to not go for the hard sell straightaway and open the video by talking about your product and how it has helped or will help the audience. That way you are taking the sales conversation out of the picture, however, always put a call to action at the end. Viewers will be keen to know what they should do once they finish watching your video. Tell them and make it easy for them to take the next step.

PERSONAL STORY: This is commonly called guest posting but personal stories have been featured for a lot longer in traditional media. It is one of the best ways to create a personal brand. This is where you write a personal story and send it to the editor explaining the "why" behind writing this piece. These pieces are hugely worthwhile if you are sharing an experience that readers will relate to, especially readers in your area of expertise. These types of posts can be list-based, experience-based, a reaction to something but the one thing that makes them different from the others on this list is that they are more personal. You will need to be comfortable talking about yourself and your experience in this type of publicity format.

As well as online, keep an eye for human-interest sections and features in newspapers and popular magazines. I would encourage you to look at popular magazines as a way of researching what works well. Magazines are an excellent way of getting coverage for this type of story because they are always looking for stories that resonate strongly with their readership, and if strong enough, they will consider it for the cover. You will often see "regular people" featured in these magazines and their story attracts attention because it has a strong human-interest angle.

Examples:

- How a Peppa Pig funfair inspired me to lose weight
- My holiday nightmare with my in-laws and what I learned about myself
- My husband told me on our honeymoon that we would need a lawyer when we got home
- 5 business mistakes I wouldn't wish on my worst enemy
- So, you hate how you look on Zoom? Here are 5 tips on how to change this

They don't have to be hard hitting. Do you have a personal story you are willing to share? If someone comes to me and is interested in doing this, I always encourage them to take their time and tell it from the heart. Don't think about how it could or couldn't get publicity or think about writing it this way or that way. The more natural it is, the better. Write it as you feel it. Guest posts, and in particular personal stories, are great ways to get publicity, because you are taking off the mask of "the businessperson" and just being you. You are naturally taking the sales talk out of conversation because you are being more personal. However, when people connect with your story, they will be keener to follow you and find out how you can help them.

Next time you are at the dentist, spend some time flicking through these magazines if you can. In there, people share their personal stories, and many have gone on to get further media coverage and book deals as a result of getting featured in there. And sometimes, publications pay for personal essays so keep an eye out for these opportunities too.

CUSTOMER STORY: Why not pitch your story from the customer's point of view? You know that customer whose life was transformed because they used your service or product? Approach that person and ask them if they would do this. Before you go down this route, I always urge some caution, as you need to pick someone who is essentially going to be the focal point of your business for this campaign. You need to build a good relationship with them and make sure you both are clear on what is expected from the campaign.

Having an agreement in writing is always best. Being super prepared is also advisable as you don't want to encounter problems down the line. Know exactly what you want this person to talk about and what you want them to say if they are asked any difficult questions. He or she may need some brief training on interview skills before you send them off into the world to essentially serve as a media spokesperson for you. This preparatory work will be worth it, especially if he/she is good at this and you want to include them in future work. Depending on the type of relationship you have with this person and how much you want them to do, you will need to discuss how you are going to reward/pay them for their time. For a substantial project, payment will be required as this person will be investing a lot of their time and energy into doing this job for you. It is essentially a job.

If the spokesperson is getting paid, then you need to be careful that this person states this in any online posts they do so you are transparent. Depending on the type of relationship you are creating, it is also a good idea to work through a content calendar where you help draft and construct posts for social media. Discuss whether you want them to also write posts and if you need them to be cleared by you in advance of being posted (I recommend the latter). Make sure you both are working off the same file which should be a shareable one like a Google Doc.

Customer stories work best when the person is happy to share the personal side of why they like your product or service. Construct the journey of the story together and how you want to tell it piece by piece. Discuss how long you think the campaign should run and what happens when the campaign is over, and your spokesperson gets featured in a publication. This can happen many months later when a journalist finds a previous article as part of their research. To start with, pick the outlets you want to share it with and how you want social media to help build awareness.

SOCIAL GATHERINGS: Do you host employee gatherings? A Christmas charity event? A fashion show? Do you host any type of gathering? If you look at your local newspaper or glossy magazine, you will see that social shots are a huge part of what they do. It is a way for them to grow their audience. There are some ways that you can make your social gathering even more attractive to a publication. I always recommend that you tell a publication well in advance that you are hosting a social event because they may send a photographer to cover it. To make it more enticing, you can get a local celebrity to come along to your event and stage a photo with this person, alongside a few key people in your business. Get your employees to wear a certain colour to mark a certain day, for example, pink for Breast Cancer Awareness or an event, like your local team has just won a competition so you could wear the team colours.

Don't think of these types of photos like business ones. Think of them more like being part of a social scene that is being captured on camera. Make sure all of the people in the photo know that you may be submitting it to certain outlets or that the person taking it is a press photographer. **Make sure you have their consent to be depicted holding drinks, at the bar etc.** Always take photos in which no drinks appear in any case, so you have a choice. **Take them early in the event, not at the end (photographers will be aware of this)**, when people are likely to be…less coherent, shall we say. Try to take them in a casual setting which clearly shows it is a social event, not a business meet-up.

Warning: Make sure you know the identity of literally everyone in the photo, along with why they are in the photo. Many people stand in for social photos, but you need people who are relevant to your business. At this point, I should mention the woman pictured beside a CEO who was later discovered to be his mistress (about whom his wife didn't know). He ultimately faced up to the controversy which resulted, and he resigned from his job. Just make sure you know who everyone is in the photo and why they are in it!

CHALLENGES: Approach your media outlet of choice and ask about running a challenge with them. These are great ways to get regular coverage as the challenge progresses. What is a challenge?

- Learn to cook 4 great desserts in 4 weeks
- Up style your wardrobe in 6 weeks without buying anything
- How you can be more confident by adopting one simple trick

every week for 8 weeks
- Makeover Madness – we make over 4 first-time mothers, and you can be 1!

I worked in the features department for many years, and we were always trying to come up with ideas for challenges, as these are a great way to get readers to follow along. These were particularly popular at the start of the year and during the summer months. A lot of these tend to be based around weight loss, and while these can be good, media outlets are looking for fresh ideas or a fresh take on an old idea. I was involved in doing reader makeovers for many years, and they are one of the best ways a business can get coverage. But you can create a challenge around something people need help with but that leads them to you to carry on the journey they started.

Visibility for your business on a major scale

There is a lot that can be gained from doing a challenge in partnership with a media outlet. You get the pre, during and post hype and coverage both on and offline. As a bonus, you may also get coverage on radio and television as oftentimes journalists in other outlets will want to be following a challenge that is attracting a lot of attention. And then you have the word of mouth as people talk about what they are learning from following along with the challenge. This can be a great way to allow the audience to get a deeper look at what you do. Use hashtags for your social media and encourage others to use them too. That way you can engage with those who are posting about your challenge. You may also find other stories among the challenge's participants and followers that you can highlight or pitch to journalists to keep the conversation going.

Always try to have a wrap up story at the end of the challenge and get some testimonials. It is also a good idea to pinpoint a follow-up story for 2-3 weeks after, so you let readers know any outcomes of the challenge or how you want them to proceed. Don't leave your followers hanging, let them know the next steps they should take with you. Try to ensure that any goals you are mapping into your challenge are realistic and achievable in the timeframe you've set for the challenge. If they aren't, followers will get turned off quickly. Keep in mind the time your audience has to do the challenge and the time the journalist has to devote to it. Keeping things bite-sized and easy to consume is a good thing to consider.

Build in a transformation into your challenge

So, if your business is involved, there are many ways you can get coverage by helping a reader through a challenge that transforms their life. Also, you can use your own social media platforms to highlight your specific involvement like any behind the scenes work you are doing, interviews with anyone on your team and so on. Also, get a member of your team to provide helpful tips, keep track of the reaction you are getting online and share it out to your wider audience to keep the good vibes flowing.

This is a lot of work but before you commit to being involved, you need to have someone on your team who is willing to take on the workload of being the go-to person for your participation in this challenge with a media outlet. This person will be involved in promoting both within your business and public facing via the media outlet. He/she will be the go-to person between you and the media outlet, and this is a really important role.

So, it is a lot of work and you will want to make sure you pick a time that is good for you to do this, so you maximize your efforts. To take the overwhelm out of the picture, look at this as one of your major publicity activities for the year where you are growing your audience, building relationships with the media, and bolstering your reputation.

Build in a couple of downtime days right after this challenge where you do something relaxing for yourself outside of work and if you have colleagues treat them to a lunch and the rest of the day off! Showing appreciation and gratitude will work wonders for building your likeability. Mention this at the start of the challenge so they know you are aware of the amount of effort this publicity activity requires. Note that you can do a challenge yourself without any media involvement, but if you are looking to build relationships with media and do something worthwhile for readers/listeners/viewers, then this is a great way to do that.

Best times to pitch a challenge idea

The best times to pitch these kinds of ideas to media outlets are when they are less busy – times like summer in particular August, January, February – when many sources of news are shut for holidays and the start of the new year is when journalists are always looking for something a little different or something that they can get their teeth into and start working on and promoting to their audience. If there is something new coming down the tracks in your area of business say like new legislation, something that is going to impact a lot of people, then it is a good idea to pitch a challenge or a learning week to teach people about this topic.

The start of a new year is a great time to pitch a challenge, as readers are most likely interested in trying something new around this time. Try to tie in your challenge with a time of the year. That way, the media outlet you pitch to will have another good reason to work with you on your challenge. Pitch it early so you have time to cement an agreement and build a relationship that helps you to get the most from this partnership. Also, put in place how you are going to look at the statistics and results afterwards, so you get a detailed view of what worked and what didn't. Importantly, you will know how to build on this or if this is something you wouldn't do again.

Importantly, see this as a way of building strong media relationships and not just with the media outlet you are working with on this challenge. Like I said earlier, other media outlets will be keen to cover a challenge that is garnering interest and that could also benefit their audiences.

PRODUCT PHOTOS FROM AROUND THE WORLD: Do you get people to try your product as a way of getting feedback early on in the lifecycle? If you do, you could ask these people to get a photo taken of them using the product in their location – on the beach or at a tourist hotspot. I know of multinational companies who use this type of publicity to show how popular their products are around the world. You could try it too.

If your product has been released in a new country, why not try to set up a photo with someone using it there. Then, pitch this with a short caption to your local newspaper or magazine that is specific to your area or branch out and send it into lifestyle magazines and to any reader columns. It shows audiences that you are reaching out and helping a wider customer base and this will pique their interest. Also, journalists will be interested in the photo as these are not widely used as a way of generating publicity.

PHONE-IN SHOWS: There is a radio show in Ireland called *Live Line* and it is one of the most popular in the country. It allows listeners to vent live on air. If you listen to these types of shows, you will find that there are lots of opportunities for you to help a listener and to get noticed by the media. It is also a way of knowing what are the pressing issues that are in people's minds, i.e., your potential customers. I know of many companies who have contacted a phone-in show and said that they could help a listener with their problem. The publicity they got from that, and the goodwill which followed, was priceless. No amount of advertising spend will get you this type of coverage.

My biggest tip, if you are considering this route, is to get to know the phone-in show and keep a close eye on how listeners or viewers are helped to solve their problems. Have the show on in the background at your place of work and you will start to see how valuable these types of shows can be to your publicity efforts.

Building story generation tools into your publicity

Above, I've given you many ways in which you can pitch to the media both with and without sending in a press release. Nevertheless, I often urge people to send a press release along with any of the above options as an informational tool to help the journalist decide. But this is not essential.

Look at these options as ways to cultivate a story generation culture in your business. These are also good ways to sustain publicity after initially getting featured. Keeping momentum going is key to staying relevant. You can do a lot on your own social media too in between pitching to the media.

Publicity Exercise

Over the next week, I want you to pick two routes from the list of publicity routes mentioned in this chapter which you will work on over the next 6-8 months. I want you to take action.

Please write your answers to the following:

This week, I will start to mine my own story and pick 2 publicity routes from the list mentioned above to focus on

Write down your 2 here:

This week, I will write out a reason why I have picked these 2 routes and what I need to do to start making them a reality.
Write down why you have chosen these routes here:

CHAPTER 5

THE INGREDIENTS YOU NEED

When I look at a potential story pitch, I break it down into key ingredients. These ingredients are what will turn your content into a newsworthy story. This skill is taught to journalists in college or on the job by a more senior journalist. It helps them decide whether or not your story is worthy of their time. Press releases and other forms of pitches I've received in the past often lack the very basics of what a story requires. I honestly believe it is a lack of knowledge about what a newsworthy story is that is preventing people with good stories from getting coverage.

These are the ingredients I'm talking about:

Professionalism – you need to present your media press release and/or information in a professional way. A message sent to a journalist with one or two lines explaining a story's worth doesn't cut it. Neither does an 800-word press release. Keep your press release to 500 words maximum. Present your pitch email in 4-5 paragraphs. Try not to have typos (proofread twice, and ask someone else to do it, if possible), and try not to waffle. There are exceptions and I've experienced this on more than occasion, but I don't recommend it. I once had a note sent to me on a postcard with two lines written on it in bad handwriting (it became a talking point that week in the newsroom as I discovered a good story from it). Another time, the details of a story were pasted into the subject line of an email. Typos are not the end of the world (speaking personally), but it is easy to just not have any.

Attention-grabbing – From reading the first line and headline of your release, a journalist should get all he or she needs to help make up their mind whether they will go ahead and read the rest. Ask yourself over and over, what is the most attention-grabbing part of what you are trying to say, and how can you fit this in early? This goes for your pitch, your photo caption, your challenge – everything.

Names – This may seem obvious, but this is often the thing that sets things off on the wrong foot. Get the journalist's name correct. This is an essential ingredient. Nowadays, it is easier with social media. But pre-social media, it wasn't easy, and it involved finding out information by buying a lot of newspapers and magazines or by ringing up outlets. The number of times I've received a press release addressed to a journalist in a rival newspaper is quite staggering. Such a basic lack of professionalism at the very beginning is an absolute killer. Also, use the correct names and titles in your pitch. Double-check spelling and titles.

Headline and Sub-Headline – You should try to use both of these, but one must complement the other. Your headline comes first, and then your sub-headline (which is the line of text that runs right under the headline on the page). Remember, though, that these will most likely be changed, so try to come up with a good one yourself, but don't wait too long for it to be perfect. It will get changed to suit the story the journalist will do. It will then get changed again to fit the space assigned to it online and on the page. And it may well get changed again if a page needs to be redesigned due to an advert being cancelled or added, even at the last minute, just before going to press. Apart from this, the editor may want to change it out of personal choice.

So, please don't spend a lot of time on this. Just make sure it encapsulates your story and has the latest and most pertinent information in it. Pitch Email: A pitch email needs a good introductory paragraph that is snappy and engaging. It doesn't need a headline or sub-headline. After your introductory sentence, 3-4 paragraphs after that are sufficient. Keep it in total to between 150 and 200 words maximum and in the body of the email, no attachments. Pitch emails are totally different to press releases and I will deal with this in more detail later in the book. They are written specifically with that journalist in mind, and you should address them personally.

Paragraphs of varying length – Your information should not be presented in one block. Allow for plenty of white space to make your information more readable. Highlight in bold some elements that you think are worth noting. This is all about helping the journalist understand what your story is about and most importantly getting them to understand it quickly. But don't go crazy into different-coloured fonts and using different font styles. Bold is fine but keep it to a minimum.

Guidelines and Readability – Make it easy to read and let your personality shine through. Make sure that, whatever outlet you are pitching to, you know the guidelines if they have any (many newspapers don't have guidelines as such, but it is safe to assume that they don't want reams of content, a lot of links to look up or high-definition photos that block up their inbox because the file size is so large. Always send images in a shareable file link not as attachments unless requested). Journalists want a story told to them straightforwardly and succinctly. For guest posting, there are guidelines you will need to follow like word counts and style. Check this before sending.

Quotes – These are important. But don't have a series of quotes that go on and on. Keep them short and punchy. Make them really stand out. Think of the quote as something that could possibly be used in the headline (journalists love these). Use quotes wisely and allow them to bolster what the rest of your content is saying. Have them say something important, not just anything that any spokesperson could say. Have your quotes stand out from the rest of the text in terms of what they say. I can't emphasise these points enough, but they are so overlooked. In press releases I received over the years, the quotes ran on and on and quite frankly a lot of it shouldn't have been in quotes.

My biggest tip is to look at the quotes you have and pick 1-2 sentences from it that are the strongest and that speak the loudest. Use these prominently in your release and use the rest further down but be selective.

Also, get clearance for the quotes from the person speaking on the topic and don't be afraid to edit them to make them punchier and more newsworthy. You may find that a quote may work best as the headline of the press release and this is most likely what could attract the journalist to your piece in the first place. Your quote should show personality, an opinion. It must be valuable.

Tell Your Story – This sounds simple, doesn't it? However, a media story is like no other. The story starts with the latest information or the most exciting information, as I mentioned previously, and it works back from there. Start with what is happening right now and work your way back to whatever is relevant. Don't go right back to the start unless absolutely necessary (in the majority of cases it isn't). If you do go back to the start, you will by then be looking at a press release that is much longer than 500 words, which is what I do not recommend. Be selective. Don't try to tell your whole story in one press release. Map out your content.

Stick to this:
one story = one press release

New – You must be presenting something new or a new take on an old topic. Then, explain why you are telling this story now and why you believe it is newsworthy.

Relevant – How is your story relevant to the news today? Can you make it relevant to the news today? You can only do this if you know what is going on around you locally, regionally, and internationally.

Photographs – You should include a photograph in most cases, but make sure it is a good-quality photo that relates to the release. It was okay in the past to send photos as attachments, but this isn't the case now. This is because journalists are receiving hundreds of emails every day and links to photos work best. Don't become that person that has clogged up their inbox (instant delete if you do that). Let them ask you for more photos if they are needed. Have low and high-resolution available so if they do decide to do your story, they can quickly look at the low-resolution ones and go back to download the one they want in high-resolution at a later time without ever having to contact you. A good headshot is fine if you don't have anything else. But you should always be working on your collection of images for media material.

I encourage you now to do an inventory of the images you have for publicity and ask yourself these six questions:

- Do these photos reflect my business as it stands now?
- Do they capture me in a happy moment?
- Do they tell a story?
- Is there any action in the photo?
- Am I happy with these being printed or posted up online?
- Do I need to go back to the drawing board and get new images done?

You may find that the journalist will send a photographer to take a certain photo that they want. But they might never consider doing this if they didn't have some sense of you from the photos you've already shown them. This can be as simple as them looking at the type of photos you have on your website. Journalists need to think visually as well.

Speaking Skills – Are you or the person quoted ready to speak to a journalist if he/she calls? Are you ready to do a sit-down interview? Are you knowledgeable enough to field wide ranging questions about issues in your area? Are you happy to go to a newsroom and be interviewed there, or would you prefer to meet in a café or your own office? Know the answers to these questions or at least have preferences to some before you make your submission.

Celebrity – Are you working with a celebrity or someone well known in your area? This should be a central part of your quest for coverage. Have a written agreement in place with your celebrity before embarking on publicity. Don't rely on a verbal agreement (More on this later).

Launch – Are you launching anything? A book, restaurant product, product-line, business premises, etc.? If so, this should be central to your release. For a launch, you should give yourself at least a 5-6-month window ahead of the launch date to work on publicity and drum up excitement. I can't count the number of times I've read a press release or other form of pitch to find out only at the very end that it involves a launch with a major celebrity within a matter of days. And that's only counting those I've read until the very end. This information should be at the top of your release. If you are working with a celebrity, you need to get maximum value from your investment. Working well ahead of time opens up more possibilities.

Contact details – The word "ENDS" should be at the end of your press release (see chapter on press release writing for more detail). This signifies that everything above this word can be used. All below it are notes and your contact details – your boilerplate. Make sure the person whose contact details are included is available for calls. You may get quite a few, and there is nothing worse than a journalist having to ring someone countless times to get an interview. Again, it's unprofessional, not to mention frustrating for a journalist. Always remember if you are not ready, someone else will be.

This might all seem complicated and time-consuming but take a deep breath. You don't have to have all of this mastered early on and you don't need all of these elements starting off. I know many businesses that only master two or three of these elements, and they get on just fine with media outlets. This is mainly because they are reliable and trustworthy, they know when to send a pitch and when they feel a journalist should know about something. They are also ready to discuss it with the journalist and further develop the story with more research, quotes etc.

If I had to pick three of the most important ones, then these are the ones I'd focus on first.
 - Having a professional approach - don't pitch until you're ready
 - Laying out your story with the pertinent detail on top
 - Headline and Sub-Headline
 - Getting good quotes - these bring personality to your story and give

the journalist something to focus on. If you start there, the rest will follow with time.

Regarding photographs, people sometimes spend a lot of money getting photos done professionally, only to realise that at the end of it all, the media outlet prefers to take their own photos. It is impossible to know this before you start so of course you are going to get your own taken. But don't get disheartened if they don't use the photos that you sent in. They will still be useful to other outlets, online and as a useful tool that shows you are a professional brand and business.

Also, when this happens and they don't use what you sent them, this is where you need to study the issue. This is when you should sit down to look at the photos you sent in and compare them to what was used. Spot the differences and save a copy of the article for future reference. **Always save copies of your coverage and look over them when you next pitch to a media outlet.** You will be surprised how your knowledge grows and how you learn so much about pitching to the media via first-hand study and experience.

All of the above ingredients are important to build your professionalism as a media pitcher. Whenever I work with someone, I ask them to look at their goals for publicity by analysing the ingredients they feel they have and listing those they don't have, then determining how they are going to get them.

Don't pitch a half-baked story and expect the journalist to fill in the rest. They won't – simple as that. It is your job to have the pitch as good as it can be and then start a conversation about how you and the journalist can work together to get it featured. **It is a collaborative relationship – never forget that.** In the next chapter, I show you what it is like to be in the journalist's seat when they get your email.

CHAPTER 6

WHAT YOU SEE AND WHAT I SEE - INSIDE THE NEWSROOM

Answer these three questions:

- When was the last time you read a newspaper, whether a physical copy or an online copy?
- When was the last time you listened to the news?
- When was the last time you watched daytime television or any other magazine-type show?

If you have answered no to all of these, you need to address the situation and start engaging with the media. If you have answered yes to more than one, you are on the right track, but you need to build on this. Before you pitch a story to a media outlet, you need to get serious about reading articles and listening to or watching shows that you want to pitch to. Start with ones you like but only if they serve your purpose and if they have a section that you can pitch to.

So many businesses do not do this research, and they fail straight off, all because they are pitching to the wrong places. You need to pick the outlets that are looking for content you can deliver. Do this first before you even think about your pitch. I guarantee that this research will inform your pitch in a massive way and in a way that will make it easier for you to become successful.

IMPORTANT TIP: Do not batch-send your press pitch. It is obvious to a journalist when you do this, and it will result in time wasted on an activity that will not reap rewards. Narrow down your focus first. Get to know what you can pitch and to who and then get ready to send out your content.

So many get their content together first and then blast it out everywhere. This is still common practice which baffles me. You need to be able to tailor your pitch to the media outlet and journalist you are sending to. I'm not saying you need to rewrite everything. You don't need to do that. You need to tailor it. You will only know how to do this by doing this research first.

Research first, story after.

Start local

If this is one of the only things you remember from reading this book, I'll be happy. Because honestly, this so often dismissed by many as the "slow route", but it can open doors to bigger outlets a lot more easily and quicker, yet many don't realize this. Many businesses are happy with having a good relationship with their local journalists and they don't need or want any more than that. And they know that if their story is worthy of national attention, the local journalist will pitch it because locals and nationals are always in touch with one another.

Sometimes when a local journalist doesn't pitch a story to a national publication, it may still get picked up by a national reporter because they are always looking for stories in local issues that they can use themselves. The best part of this for you is that you won't have to lift a finger and do any hard grafting once they story appears locally. If it is a good story, it will travel and reach a wider audience, and this will be doubly amazing – **you get the publicity and you get it by nurturing just a small few relationships locally.**

But before you get excited and rush off to send emails to every local outlet (sorry but I need to say this), hold your horses! Yes, this is a wonderful journey to take but you first must do your homework and set aside time to get familiar with outlets in your local area. Then AND only then should you start to send in your story. Start small and build relationships with 1-3 key people. Then and only if you feel the need, you can work your way towards the bigger outlets, armed with some clippings from local publications.

When you have mastered the local publicity scene and would like to grow from there, then start by doing the same study of national publications that cover your area. By studying both local and national, you'll be able to see the difference between how they cover stories. And this is a vital skill to have and one you can learn by just being open to learning and seeing the angles that are taken on stories.

What makes an impact

You'll start to realise that what could make an impact with a local outlet wouldn't have a hope of doing so with a larger one, and vice versa. That is why having a journalist locally pitch it to the nationals is the best because if they believe enough in the story, they will do their best to help it get featured both for their benefit and for spreading a good story. At the end of it all, journalists believe in storytelling and they have an instinct (most do) for when a story needs a wider audience. So many local journalists freelance for nationals. Once you invest in a local relationship, believe me, you will start to see benefits but invest the time and be patient. But always persevere.

One of the biggest mistakes I see when I work with people is that they haven't taken the time to find out anything about the local media scene around them. They are thinking they need to get featured in national and household name publications to make an impact. If you haven't guessed by now, I am a big believer in starting local. This is where you will learn the ropes, learn what it takes to build a media relationship, and it is where you can make mistakes without having the world and their mother know about it. And best of all, they will be your biggest champions when it comes to telling your story if they deem it worthy of national attention.

Questions you should be able to answer about your local scene:

- What are the local newspapers, magazines, radio, and television shows in your area?
- Do you know the names of journalists in those titles?
- Are you following any of them online?
- Who is the business editor in those outlets?
- Who is the news editor?
- Who is the features editor?
- Who writes about what your area?
- What past articles have they written about your area? What angle excited them?
- What opinions do they have on any issue in your area?

Try to build up a picture of the journalist's likes, dislikes, and interests.

Also:

- Do you know who the overall managing editor in any of these outlets is?
- Is he/she a part of any local organisation you are also a member of?

Look at the media outlet in terms of sections

Take a look at the sections in these outlets – do you know if they do Q&A type pieces that are open for submissions. They will often have an email you can send your details to underneath. These are often part of a lifestyle, entertainment, or business section where the publication profiles a person. The questions are often the same every week so there is a formula that is followed by the journalist, making it easier for them to collate the information and it is also easier for you. You will get to see what questions are asked and you can in advance think of interesting answers that will help you stick out more. And for the readers, this is a quick read, something many readers enjoy and find value in because they can dip and out of a publication, pick up an article, read it quickly and feel they got something for their time.

For some, this is their first experience of a media outlet and dealing with a journalist. This is where they answer the series of set questions and the feature appears pretty close to what you submitted. It is often a good place to introduce yourself. You will normally find the email to contact and send in your request to be included at the bottom of these columns. Be sure to send in an email that has some personality, reasons why you think you would be a good fit for the column and anything you like about it to show you've been reading it.

Look for other sections like:

Do they do a round-up of tweets of the week? Photos from events A behind the scenes piece about a product/service - a profile piece Fashion Out and About - style from the streets Break down the outlet into sections as this makes it so much easier to mark out where you think your story could fit.

Look at fitting your story into the outlet in two ways:

- As a story that is of value to the audience that needs your area of expertise

- As a story that can be related to the wider news agenda

One of the reasons many people don't get a response to their email is because it is obvious that they don't have any knowledge of the publication and how their story fits in with what they do. By pitching to a column or section like I've mentioned above, you are giving yourself a good first opportunity to get featured and build relationships. This is an easy way in and one you should consider.

Combating overwhelm

How do you combat that feeling of wanting to start but feeling overwhelmed by it all? This can be a lot of work, but it doesn't have to be overwhelming past the point of implementation. So, here is what I want you to do first.

Don't worry about your pitch. Just read, watch, and listen. Pay attention to what is working for others in your area, what piques your interest as an audience member and as someone who wants to get featured. Take some notes along the way. You will get better at taking these notes once you gain knowledge and you will start to recognise how you could fit in. This will help make the process less overwhelming and something you are building at your own pace.

I recommend starting with the easier ones first like a local magazine, newspaper, radio station or television show. Then cast your net wider as you gather information. This research will help to inform you how to pick shows, newspapers, and magazines that you would like to get featured and most importantly you'll know how to get started. You will have the most important information - what these media outlets like to cover.

By doing this, you will eventually begin to hone your focus to the areas that relate to you and that represent opportunities for publicity. You will eliminate sections and shows that don't fit your purpose right now. Keep your list, though, as you just never know when you might pitch to one of the other shows in future. Listen to the daytime shows, the late-night shows, the morning radio shows. Start picking up newspapers, and analysing the front pages, followed by the pages inside, noting what kind of content appears on each page number. You will see patterns emerge. There is a well-developed science behind the layout of newspapers and magazines. I won't go into it here, but designers have an instinct to know where photos would work best, where stories should sit on the page. Editors too have this skill that is mostly acquired on the job and by doing it day after day, week after week.

Immerse yourself and document your research

This can be a really enjoyable time for your business and as the picture of opportunities starts to come together, you will start to see all the exciting places you can pitch to. Remember too that by doing this you are building the most valuable piece of collateral in your PR. You don't have to go out and buy loads of newspapers. A lot of libraries have newspapers and magazines available for free, so go there first if you don't want a load of newspapers lying around your office or home. Sign up for a free subscription to get the first episode/publication for free or get that television subscription working for you by watching shows that are going to help build PR for your business.

In my experience, there will be a moment down the road when you'll remember something someone said, a problem from a listener or presenter, a television or radio slot that didn't suit you back then but does now and you'll know where and how to send in your pitch or press release. You'll have this document as your reference point. I'll deal more with sending out press releases and pitches later in this book. But, for now, enjoy this time. Immerse yourself. Look at it as research and uncovering the many publicity opportunities that are out there to pitch to.

A journalist knows if you have read the newspaper or watched/listened to their show. They know by your pitch, the type of story you are pitching, when you pitch, how you pitch, the language you use, even down to the person you address it to. So, remember this as you do this research.

Why you can't pitch the same story to the locals and the nationals

What to look for when you are studying a local outlet also applies to a national publication too. But you can't pitch the same story to both and here's why.

What is being done locally will need a different focus if it is to be covered nationally. This is important to note. However, a lot of local stories do make national headlines, and if you notice this, you need to understand how the story began in a local media outlet and was developed to be newsworthy in a national outlet. This is a hugely important learning curve. What is suitable for local isn't always suitable for national – unless it is packaged in such a way that makes it national, worthy of a bigger audience and has a wider appeal.

I think looking at it this way helps a lot. For a local, you can concentrate on the angle that is most newsworthy to the local audience, the people who live around you. For a national, you need to have a wider angle on your story, zoom out and see it from the point of view of a wider range of people or how it impacts a sector, how it relates to a running story, or an initiative or programme that impacts a large number of people.

Journalists working at the local and national levels look at each other's work. They know whether the story will work from a local to a national and vice versa. They are keen to get stories and do follow-ups. Just because you featured in a local outlet, it doesn't mean it may not get picked up by a national one. But you will need to know that to make your local story of interest to the nationals, you will need to make it worthy of a larger audience.

Inside the newsroom

Let me give you an inside view of what it is like working in a newsroom. For me, knowing this will set you apart from others who don't take the time to know a little about what it is like to work as a journalist. I'll first give you an insight into how newsrooms looked when I started off. However, I also want you to be aware of how things have changed in traditional media with outlets older than 100 years closing down in recent years. This is a sad development, but it is one that has brought on new ways of doing things. Many journalists will openly tell you that online quickened the pace of change that was inevitable many years ago. Having said that, newsrooms still exist, and the story remains the most important thing.

When I started off, prior to social media, the newsroom was not just for journalists. There were also photographers, designers, editors (many different levels here: sub-editors, headline writers but the main editor had a separate office). Next to the newsroom were advertising executives and all of their management team, along with marketing and public relations, human resources, accounts, and higher management. Sometimes, there is a need to call in a legal team before a story is run, but it is rare that there is a legal department on-site in a publication. The hub of any news outlet is its newsroom, the characters within it and how they work together.

And what has become rare is the need to have a printing press on site. In the 1990s, it was common that each newspaper had their own printing press or shared one, and they would use this to print not only the newspaper but also any other news titles, supplements, booklets, and any major print jobs requested by customers. Some even did wedding invites, bereavement cards, mass cards and bookmarks. So, it was profitable to have a printing press on site. But as the online world has changed so much within the media world, newspapers and magazines outsource this or they are part of a group that prints publications all in the one place. There are of course those that don't print at all.

Why do I go into such detail on this? Because if the newspaper or magazine you are sending to has to get their printed issues back from a printing press on the other side of the country, then their deadline will need to fit in things like the time it takes to print, their time slot and the time it takes to get the issues distributed. This impacts greatly on your story in particular if you are dealing with a story on deadline day.

The newsroom today

The job of the journalist has changed a lot since I started. As well as writing for the publication itself whether print or online, fresh content is needed for social media, the website, and for Instagram stories. The job was always a pressurised one but nowadays, the pressure is even more intense. Add to that the growing number of publications that have had to close their doors or let people go. And the journalists that are left are finding themselves with more work to do. Sadly, some stories don't get done.

This is an opportunity, not something to turn away from. News outlets have responded to this by reaching out more to those who share content like bloggers, beauty influencers, estate agents providing good content on their site, people around them who have good content to share. News outlets have had to adapt and partnerships with others are becoming more common. This is where you can put your helpful hat on and start to add value on your own platform first, and then pitch stories that fit their needs while showing links to copy you've already written. Helping a journalist do their job is one of the best ways to look at how publicity works. Base your content on a strong story and you'll get their attention.

Let's go back inside the newsroom. It is a full-on busy place. That's one aspect the films have got right. Everyone in it is striving to do one thing – to break the latest big story and have the best coverage. In the daily grind that is newspaper journalism, newsroom staff are scrambling around waiting for print-offs of stories to edit while asking a journalist for their story, as there is only five minutes left before he/she needs to read it and edit it. It is very fast-paced, and it is the norm sometimes for journalists to skip lunch or stay late to work on stories. It is not a 9-5 job. A lot of newsworthy events happen in the evening, so journalists might be working a full day and going straight from the office to an event that night.

In the newsroom, journalists bounce ideas off each other, come up with headlines, and discuss press releases and pitches that have been sent in. Once in a while, journalists gather around a colleague's computer to see a release that has something unique or a photo that just says it all. There is a camaraderie there, and you need to understand that journalists talk all the time. This includes reporters in other newspapers, even their biggest competitors (shock, horror!).

You also need to be aware of other areas your targeted journalist covers. Be patient. I did a lot of feature writing but during the day and I spent a lot of time in court rooms. Expecting me to be by my phone or respond to an email during the day showed me that people didn't know what I did. Be aware that journalists nowadays have a lot on their plates.

How this impacts your approach

If the newspaper has a small team, it will take longer for them to get back to you. Hence, it will take longer for your story to get written and appear in the media outlet. You'll need to figure this into your timeline and make sure you pitch your story early. Give yourself at least 3 weeks before you need publicity for your story if you want to get featured in a local paper, 3 months for a national, and even longer for a national supplement, and for major magazines like art or business. In the latter cases, give yourself a minimum of 4 months because it is extremely competitive and like I said earlier you need to build relationships first before you can expect your story to be featured.

But I always say that if your story is a breaking one, has a unique angle and just has to be told, this all goes out the window the moment the journalist receives it. **A good story takes precedence over everything** and for exclusives editors will hold their printing slot or hold off putting it online until they know the story has enough details to make a major impact. There is a lot that goes on behind the scenes that the general public has no knowledge of and doesn't need to know. Unless, that is, you are looking for publicity. It is good to have some insights, so when you email a media outlet, you have some idea of what's going on, and this will come across in your pitch.

Links between departments

In the days of journalism prior to social media and during my first years, the editorial department and the advertising department were strictly separate in terms of doing our jobs. An advertiser would not be putting pressure on a journalist to do a story on a product or service. Although an advertisement might sometimes spark a story idea, the two existed independently. Or a story might spark an advertisement, or even a supplement, if a business wanted to capitalise on something that had become topical. An advertising executive would be the judge of that. The lines between these two departments have become more blurred in recent years and while as a media person I can understand why, my heart has always been in journalism and it being independent of everything. But I'm afraid that topic is for another book!

Just so you know there will be times when getting a story featured will be reliant on you spending some money on advertising. This is becoming a more regular occurrence now with newspapers struggling to survive and trying to maintain operations. However, this isn't always the case, especially if you pitch your story in a newsworthy way to a journalist you have a good relationship with. Like I said early, newspapers and other media outlets are changing how they do things and generating revenue like their online counterparts as this has become necessary for some to survive.

If an advertiser wants to put in an editorial piece, then it should be labelled "Advertorial". This way, readers know what they are reading. On the other hand, a big advertiser might put pressure on a newspaper not to run a story, threatening to pull all their advertising if the story is published. This isn't something I want you to think a lot about, but I do want you to be aware of the links that exist between advertising and getting a story published.

Think like a journalist to get their attention

To get the attention of a journalist, you need to think like one and try to put yourself in their shoes. So please, try to follow some of the points below. It will help you stand out from others who pitch.

Here's how you can do this:

- Don't pitch on deadline day

- Find out when deadline day is (it is the day before the paper comes out. For daily newspapers, it's usually late on the night before the issue comes out. Keep up to speed on deadlines and double check them regularly).

- Focus on the lead-in time the journalist needs to do your story. Some magazines and newspapers plan their Christmas content as early as August. Some magazines have 3-5 months of a lead-in time. Always plan out your coverage with as much time as you can give yourself to get featured. Find out what they cover – if they cover courts or do business features, they won't be at their desk all the time.

- Read some of their work and mention something about it in your pitch. Ideally something that resonated with you and your work or that connects in some way. Follow them on social media for a while. Comment on their work. Get to know what interests them.

- Pitch early in the morning, not the night before, because your email will go way down the list, as many will come in during the evening and night and push yours out of sight.

- Pitching on a quiet day is best (the day after the paper comes out, the day after the show is aired). However, quiet days are few and far between these days, but this is still a good tactic.

- Monday morning is one of the best times to pitch. As well as being the start of the week, it is also a time when journalists are keener to hear about new stories before their week is taken over by diary markings and other events and deadlines.

- Have an interesting subject line – don't put "Press Release" in the subject line – use this space wisely. A journalist knows that you are about to pitch to them. They are always pitch-ready. I would encourage you to not use Press Release in the subject line.

- Put a relevant subject area like "Pregnancy" or "Dieting" or put "reaction to" or put "Follow-up to".

For example:

Meditation: A mom of 3 meditates with her children before bringing them to school every day.

For a journalist that does health and lifestyle content, this is of potential interest to them. As a journalist receiving this, I am already thinking of the photos I could get, the quotes from the children, the reason why this mom does this as anyone who has kids will know that getting them ready to go anywhere takes a lot of time and energy. Why add meditation into the mix?

You've got the journalist to open the email by grabbing their interest. Don't waste valuable space in the subject line with Press Release: Story about meditation. Give something of value and of interest in the subject line. You see here how the first one gives enough to increase your chances of getting it opened. Remember, the journalist is receiving hundreds of emails every day.

- Don't put "Breaking News" in the subject line unless it involves any of the following – someone has been shot dead, a bomb has gone off, you've just witnessed a kidnapping or a robbery, someone has just jumped from a building, or there is a fire. You get the idea. Your concert is not breaking news. Neither is your art exhibition, your product, your special offer or your book tour. If you put Breaking News in your subject line for any of these, it will be deleted.

- Don't keep ringing about whether your press release will get featured. By all means, follow up, as things get missed. Follow-up with an email three days later for nationals, a week later for locals or 10 days later for trade magazines. If you still don't get a response, call a week later and if you still don't get featured, simply accept that this time at least, your content is not what they are looking for. Don't pester journalists. This is not a good look for you and your business, and it is an unethical practice that you don't want to get known for.

To call or not to call

Okay, this is a major talking point among journalists. When I worked as a journalist, I hated those calls that started with "It's a lovely day, what's the weather like there?" I'm under pressure and this person wants to first distract me and now talk about the weather. This, for me, personally, was not a good approach. And then there was the newbie PR person who was assigned a list of calls to make, and they needed to ask me and others "Did you get my press release?" Depending on the time I had I would go to look for said press release in my emails or I would politely say "Yes I got it, but I don't have time to do anything with it right now. If I am going to do something, I will get back to you." I didn't enjoy these calls or being cold-called by people who didn't have a relationship with me or hadn't tried to build one at the very least.

What I did find useful though was when a business or PR person I knew would ring to tell me why they felt a story was worth my attention. The call started with value. It had a purpose. It wasn't about buttering me up or being salesy. It was about a story that this person, who I had a relationship with, felt that I should cover. And I would listen to these calls. There were times when I was thankful that the business or PR person called me because I would have missed a good story. These are people who started off by pitching stories to me and by connecting with me at an event or on social media. They made a connection first.

Pick your calls wisely

Don't cold call a journalist. If you feel you need to call a journalist you haven't built even a small relationship with then make sure you have something else to add to the story you've already sent in, a different angle, approach or an interview to offer. Have something of value. A good way to do this is to email the journalist first and ask if it is okay to call them (he/she may not respond but at least you have given them a heads-up). Explain in the email why you feel a call would be worth their time because the story is of value to readers.

Always remember that journalists now are extremely time poor. Those days of liquid lunches, celebrity launches, wine receptions – they are no longer the reality for most. Think long days and nights in newsrooms being under pressure to get stories done, to get information for these stories and to write them in a way that is engaging. Think high stress. So, if you are going to call, you need to be mindful of this. When you have a good relationship with a journalist and you have helped them in the past with stories, you are in a better position to call. But don't abuse this. It is easy to erode a relationship with a journalist but not so easy to build one. Always remember the work you put in to build it and if that call is worth making.

Ask yourself:

- Why am I calling?
- What do I have to offer?
- Is this urgent enough to warrant a call?

Take a moment to think about it and then make your decision. If you are calling, then a week later is fine (depending on your own deadline too of course). What I encourage you to do before you call is to look at the recent issues and see if any major stories were covered. Get an idea of what was happening in the news cycle around the time you were pitching your story. If a major election happened, a major event, a popular figure in your area passed away, then note that your story didn't make it because of this, and you should consider holding off on making this call. What you should try to do next is regroup, get another story together or tweak the old one sufficiently enough and send it in again.

- Give yourself plenty of time to get their attention. Don't put yourself in a position where you have only a week to get your content in. If you allow yourself extra time, you can work on your pitch and send it in again.
- Be careful about who you ask for feedback. National journalists will not do this because they simply don't have the time, but you may be surprised by the kindness of local journalists who may tell you exactly where you are going wrong. But don't expect this. It is not their job to tell you what is wrong with your PR pitch. However, if you have built a relationship, they may let you know what works best or where they feel your story might fit better in a future supplement or feature (When I had time and felt that a little guidance would really help someone, I would do it). See, again how important local journalists can be to your publicity journey!
- Be ready for negative feedback and for lots of rejection. This is par of the course.

First time luck - it can happen but not often

You will most likely not be successful the first time you pitch. This is normal, and your first pitch rarely lands you coverage. Don't lose confidence in yourself. You can only learn in this game by experiencing it and making occasional mistakes. Learning from them is what makes you a better media pitcher. Every experience with a media outlet builds your knowledge, confidence, and resilience.

Persistence is something journalists admire. I certainly did. Journalists know all too well how being persistent is vital if one is going to survive in the cutthroat world of the media. However, you can get lucky with your first pitch if the story is a standout one that is offering a unique take on an issue, a surprise, a celebrity endorsement, or a controversial stance. But don't expect it even then. There is so much more to it like timing, space, and the journalist's diary of stories for that day or week. I have seen first-time pitches get great coverage but what I noticed most of all is that it was planned meticulously, and the business or person had their army of champions ready to keep the story in the news once it appeared in the press. There was a strategy for each social media outlet to support their media feature. Something you should consider getting in place before you send in your story.

CHAPTER 7

GENERATING IDEAS

It is a little easier to get publicity when you have something to announce, but what do you do if you don't have a launch or a new product to celebrate but your business needs some media coverage? This is when you will need to generate ideas, and it is important to look at all aspects of your business and your life to get some good ones. This is where the development of a story generation culture within your business comes into its own.

To develop ideas, there are a few things you can do. Later in this chapter, there is an extensive list of prompt questions to generate ideas.

Before we go there, I'd like you to take a moment to think about how you want to communicate this with your team. You want them to be open with you about potential stories they see could work but you don't want them to feel like they need to open up so you can grow the business. Communicate why you are asking these questions.

- Do you need visibility for a new product?

- Do you need to grow awareness for the business?
- Is there a strong competitor and you now need to prove to existing customers and potential ones that you are still the leader in this area?

It is so important to state clearly why you are now upping your media publicity efforts. That way, you will garner their support and with time they will share their story ideas. The best way to start is by leading by example.

Start with you. You can mine the story of your business for ideas, your wins and losses and your personal story. This is where personal branding can play a huge role in your business. You can start to grow your own personal brand and by getting featured, you are showing the way and being open. Having a strong personal brand is beneficial as you grow your media presence. Doing this involves being willing to share some personal stories about your life and what you've encountered in your business. Building your personal story and sharing some behind the scenes content about your life will help you become more relatable to journalists and to readers. And it will show employees that you are willing to go first and put yourself out there to generate publicity.

Become a seasonal pitcher

I have worked with businesses who only pitch at seasonal times of the year. But they prepare meticulously for these times because they know that many others will be doing the same. Before we dive deeper, let's look at what it means to be a seasonal pitcher. It means that you need to think of the media in terms of seasons/major times of the year. Audiences expect certain things at different times of the year and journalists know they need to deliver. Christmas,

Halloween, Summer, New Year, Easter. If you are struggling to come up with ideas, then look at your content and see if you can tailor it to a time of year. Link your Christmas story to an end of year round-up (lists work well) or pitch a story about the special way you reward staff or customers.

During summertime, think of how you are freshening up your business, and see if there are any new trends in your area. Do you have any data to support your reasons for doing any new business activity? Think of what your customers would most likely want at different times of year and tailor your publicity to that.

Other times of the year

While you can get ideas to coincide with popular times of the year, you won't always want to wait until such times come around to get publicity. You will want to be able to pitch a story at any time of the year. You'll need the skills to find stories, and you'll need to know what the best hook or angle is for that story. One of the most important skills is knowing when you have a good story. I would consider this one of the top skills to have when seeking publicity. And you can actually get pretty good at this by watching the news and reading stories published in your area of expertise. But also look at the unusual angle. For example, you could pitch a day-in-the-life piece of your CEO or pitch an angle about any interesting hobby he/she has. Don't dismiss these segments as ones that are outside of your area. These can often be the ones that lead to more requests for features or interviews.

I hope you have followed my earlier suggestion and have or are planning to take time away to think about publicity ideas. As a mini refresh, I suggest you first take an overall look at your business and write down things that come to mind straightaway. Don't analyse them yet; just write them down. Let your mind wander for a bit and free write.

Questions to Prompt Ideas

Now, consider the following: This is a long list but dip in and out at times when you need inspiration.

WHEN

- First, get your dates and write them down. When did you set up the business? The day, date, month, and year. Get birthday together of key employees and see if they coincide with anything in your calendar or something newsy that happens that day.

- Are you celebrating a special anniversary next year? Or in the next five years?

- Did you set up just before Christmas or on Valentine's Day, or the first day of summer?

- Is the time of your setting up of any significance? For a number of years Guinness held an event based called Arthur's Day. And at 17.59pm on the last Friday of September, everyone raised a pint of Guinness to toast Arthur, the founder of the company. (Guinness was founded in 1759). Arthur's Day revolved around this time, and their marketing was excellent (I would encourage you to check out their marketing campaigns). The day is no longer celebrated, but this was a way to get bars and restaurants all over Ireland involved and ensure people knew more about the company's origins. It also helped Guinness to cement even stronger relationships with bars, clubs, and restaurants.

WHY

- Why did you set up the company?

- What did you see in the market that needed to be changed?

- Did something happen globally that caused you to set up? A crash or a boom?

- Did you inherit the business?

- Whether you did or didn't inherit it, look back at your family tree and see if there are some interesting personalities there. This is a great way to generate ideas that people can relate to. **Examples:** The grandfather who invested his last pennies to set up a business. The grandaunt who was one of the first businesswomen in your area to set up a motor or engineering business. Did these people get publicity at the time? Could you look it up in your local newspaper's archives and see what was said? As well as contacting your local newspaper this way, you could pitch to that newspaper, stating that you have used some archival detail from their records in your press release (this will grab their interest). I encourage businesses to use the archive in their local newspaper as a way of creating historical context and seeking out inspiration for stories from things like old adverts, stories, picture spreads, headlines. So much inspiration can begin from looking in archival material in your local newspaper.

Employees and/or collaborators

- Is your very first employee still working with you? You may not realise it, but it is an amazing achievement if your first employee is still with you after a period of 5+ years or more or if you have someone working with you for decades. Millennials are keen to move on after three years, it has been reported, so if you have an employee who is still there after various ups and downs, consider whether you could ask him/her if it would be possible to do a story around this. You may glean some useful information by talking to this person and asking why they still enjoy working with the company. You could pitch it to business section, and it could form the focus of a piece about retaining employees and what you have done over the years to maintain good relationships.

• Have you formed a valuable collaboration? How did you do that? What is the story behind it and how do you make it work? Can you do something together as an offer at a time of year that celebrates your partnership?

You

• What about you? Have you ever told your story to the press?

• Did you put off doing something in your life to start a business?

• Did you ever imagine that your business would still be here after such a long time? Or after a particularly difficult start?

• Did you sell your business? And start another? Or pivot in a new direction? You see stories all the time about for example the teacher who started modelling in her 40s. Another example is the nightclub owner who decided to become a monk.

• Where did your business acumen come from?

Building rapport

- How does your business celebrate various milestones in the year?

- Do you celebrate Christmas differently? If you don't, should you start?

- Do you commemorate deceased employees in any way?

- Do you do anything for those in the office on Valentine's Day? I know a florist who gave all of his employees Valentine's Day off so they could do something nice for themselves and their partners/children. He asked the local university if he could get some volunteers with retail experience to help. Considering this is the busiest day of the year for florists, this was a huge gesture to his employees, and one that was appreciated. He also got some good coverage from it too.

- Do you do any charity work? This is an angle that is well-trodden by businesses, and that is because it remains a good one. I suggest that you try to bring a different angle to your charity work. For instance, you could approach a lesser-known charity and see if they would like your help. Or tie your business into an issue that is emerging like our water crisis or climate change.

Look forward in your business

- Apart from looking at the present and the past, what about looking forward? Is there anything exciting coming down the line for the business that you can share with the public? If not now, can you share it in three or six months, and plan a content strategy around this? It doesn't have to be something you create. It can be about a new regulation coming into the industry and how it impacts businesses, the phasing out of something, a new technology.

- I suggest that you put a calendar up in the canteen or online and ask staff to write in dates that relate to them, detailing why. Ask them for suggestions for publicity. Your employees could be doing amazing things outside of the office and you could collaborate with them on a publicity campaign.

Competitors

- Check out your competition – what are businesses in your area and outside your area but close to your niche doing to get publicity? Do any of them have a weekly or monthly column, a radio slot, or a guest television slot? Chart their journey. None of these things are out of reach for you. If this is something you would like to pursue, then you need to build up your clippings. Rather than sending in a cold pitch asking to be a contributor or have a guest slot in a media outlet (they won't answer you, because they don't know you), you should start your publicity journey first and focus on getting coverage.

After you've got some substantial coverage, you can ask if there are any guest slots or any columns that they might be interested in getting your input for. When you pitch, you will be in a position to send in your past clips. The booking agent for the show might already know you and want to work with you. Editors work with people they know and those who know how the media works.

Continue to seek out answers to the following questions:

- Is there a current story in the news right now that your business relates to? A word of warning here. You need to be ready to act now, not next week or next month. **NOW**. This news story is news today, and possibly tomorrow. It might be featured in a weekend round-up programme, but after that, it is gone. If you can relate to it, you should try to get some coverage on the angle that you can provide. You need to link it closely to the original story.

- Keep track of different themes for each month. The Superbowl is the first Sunday in February every year. March is Women's History Month. March 17 is St Patrick's Day. September is Childhood Cancer Awareness Month. By letting staff know that you are generating ideas, you may find a staff member willing to talk about their experience.

    You may find that a staff member might like to talk about their son or daughter who has cancer, as they might be trying to raise money. Instead of coming across as taking advantage of the situation by getting coverage, you can reach out to help and raise awareness of the issue. This is a way you can help your staff and also generate goodwill.

- Get a list together of the times of year you could pitch and keep this list together with your growing list of journalists that you can contact when the time is right.

Some words of encouragement

I know there is a lot to take in so far, but I want to tell you this. The most important thing is to look at your business in its present state and compare this with what it was like before and what you want it to look like into the future. I would encourage you to pick three people whose journeys you most admire and pin their photos to the wall above your workstation. Use this as encouragement to follow your media publicity dreams and to become the recognised expert in your niche.

Tap into the talents of your employees

I've tapped into this a little already, but I think it is good to focus more on it. Your employees or if you don't have any, you can look at your collaborators, could be doing amazing things outside of the office, but you would never know this unless you ask them and get to know them on a deeper level.

I worked with a business that had a staff member whose main goal was to climb 7 mountain peaks in 7 days. He was happy to tell his story, and he did a blog about preparing for the challenge, why he wanted to do the challenge, his battle with depression, and how climbing helped him get over the loss of his mother. All of this came from having a simple calendar put up in the canteen asking employees for ideas or events they were doing/involved in.

The story was covered by local newspapers and radio and was picked up by national radio and television. One tv station interviewed him as he walked down the last 100 metres of the final mountain on his challenge. He was deeply emotional about what he had achieved. The story received a lot of coverage, and it resulted in various shows both morning and evening ones discussing depression, specifically among young Irish men, who remain the most vulnerable group at risk from suicide than any other sections of the Irish population.

His manager from work along with close colleagues were there to greet him alongside his friends and family as he climbed down the last mountain. But note that this wasn't an opportunity to wave company flags or wear branded clothing. This was purely to support their colleague. The company was getting mentions and attention and there was no need to go massive on the branding for the television and radio stations. Many would be tempted to do this and go ahead and set up a welcome party full of the company colours and branding. I believe that in this instance it would not have been appropriate and in fact it would have taken away from the goodwill already generated. It would have been seen as "jumping on the bandwagon".

I want to share this story with you to show that you don't have to be directly involved in an event or to organise one to receive a boost in your visibility efforts. Support your employees and in turn this makes for a more caring working environment where the workforce can feel supported in what they do outside as well as inside work.

Keep your clippings

Always keep notes and records of what you've done. Press clippings ideally! But also, keeping clippings of stories can quicken up the process for the next time you go to pitch. You will instantly see what stories and angles worked. Also, keep the pitches that didn't work. This is a great way to generate ideas. Doing this helps to eliminate that feeling that you are starting from scratch every time you want to reach out to a publication. It also helps reduce the feeling of overwhelm that many feel at this time.

Keep it all in the one place and go to this file every now and then so you can be inspired. Look back at what you've achieved. Update it regularly. Also, keep an eye for any changes in the details – has a journalist changed jobs, do they cover a new area now or have they left journalism altogether or been laid off? Keeping your press list up to date is important because journalists tend to move around more now than they did 10 years ago or more.

Relooking at old content can spark a follow-up or a new story. It is also a way of reminding you of the resources you have. If you always do something for Valentine's Day, then you should have all of this information in a folder, so when November/December comes around again, you are ready to pull out the folder and have a list of contacts, emails, story suggestions and past clippings. Has anyone that featured in a previous story gone on to do something worthy of a follow-up?

Always keep clippings of all coverage and make sure you name them and date them. I recommend you start looking at Valentine's coverage on 1 November and start building a publicity content calendar and strategy of who you are going to pitch to and when. For example, if you are a florist, do you have anyone getting married on Valentine's Day or around this time? Would they be interested in doing some coverage with you ahead of the day and submitting a photo afterward with your flowers in the photo? By having this photo and coverage, you can have great information right there for a follow-up piece. You can get back to the couple to see what they are doing for the first anniversary; you can surprise them with flowers when they have their first child.

Celebrate your coverage

It always amazes me that people don't keep their clippings and post them and even repost them online. If you get featured, you should shout about it from the rooftops. You should have it on your website, and in your business so the public and employees can see it and be reminded of it. As businesspeople, it is easy to move on to the next thing, the next project. Take time to celebrate and enjoy your PR successes and demonstrate how much it means to your employees and/or collaborators. It encourages a story generation culture that I want you to have in your business. Getting coverage is not a one-off thing. Sadly, many do see it like this, and I encourage you to see it as a building exercise taken step by step.

When you get featured, this is the information I want you to take note of, so it helps you when you go to pitch again:

- Who did you contact?
- How many times did you have to contact this person?
- Was it a phone interview or face-to-face interview?
- How long did it take to get the piece featured?
- Was it picked up by other publications/media outlets?
- Were major changes made to the piece you sent in? Always analyse these, and this will make your pitch better next time.
- Was there anything else that you needed to do?
- Did you follow-up with another story?
- Was it published?
- Quickly search online to see if this reporter is still working at this publication and take a note of that.

You will be so thankful you did this. It will save you time and hours of searching online for information the next time you want to send out a story pitch.

CHAPTER 8

BROADCAST MEDIA AT DIFFERENT TIMES OF THE DAY

Media at different times of the day have a different focus. This is because different types of audiences tune in at different times and because it would be dull if media outlets did the same thing all day. Programmes at different times have an in-depth idea of who their audience is, and they cater to them. When you watch them, take notes on the types of segments they do. You will start to notice that morning and evening shows have a hugely different focus. The afternoon is different again. If you are pitching to a morning show, and you then decide you want to change your focus to lunchtimes or evenings, you will need to change how you pitch. You cannot pitch the same way to all of them because they have different focuses.

Once you have your pitch list, I recommend that you listen to/watch them regularly (every day if possible) for at least a week, but ideally two, before you draft your pitch. Why? Because your pitch will straightaway stand out from the crowd, because you will know about the show and the segment you want to be featured in.

Your tone will fit so much better. Many people send in a pitch to a show and expect to be placed in a segment. So many of these emails don't have a proper focus, and they get binned. If you pitch, demonstrate why you would be particularly suited to a certain segment because of a previous story that was covered there. This shows that you: watch the show, like the show to want to get featured on it and are trying to help them fill segments with newsworthy items and you know your story could fit well and would entertain their audience.

To start with, pick three. One national, one regional (a provincial title) and one local. You will start to recognise what works well at each level.

What does your breakfast time look like?

It's 7am and your alarm rises you from your slumber. What is the first thing on your mind? Okay, maybe the first is a cup of coffee or tea. But what is next? Is it a television show you watch, a radio show you listen to, or an online newspaper you read? Or do you scroll aimlessly through social media, eat your breakfast, and race out the door to your office? If you are doing the latter, you need to take a whole new look at how you spend your morning. This is the first mistake you are making if you are looking for coverage on any morning show. You need to make time to learn and listen to what programmes do in their shows at this time. I know, there are replays. But, for me, nothing beats watching it live at least once and feeling how a show operates in real-time.

Get a radio show on your phone and listen to it while on the move to work. Before you leave, carve out a half-hour time slot to watch a television show, even for only a week or two, and start reading morning news stories. If you want to get featured, you need to start becoming interested in media outlets and finding out what excites them.

One of the best ways to get featured is to react to a news story. This is termed **Reactive PR**. But news happens fast and if you are not even aware of what is making news, then you'll have no way of knowing if you can provide a follow-on story that keeps this news story alive. Journalists love good follow-on stories. Always be on the lookout to see if you can be that follow-on story. But first, you need to know what makes the news.

As you watch, listen, and read, get a feel for those that present the show and write the news, get to know the type of stories they do, and how they do them. Start following these outlets on social media. Does a presenter always mention something about his/her route to work or a favourite coffee or a favourite holiday. Try to build up a picture of them. This isn't easy I know because you don't "know him/her" but by watching the show and following them on social media (not stalking!), you will start to build a picture.

Open a Word document and start tracking the information. Here's what I'd like you to do.

When you watch a television programme, make notes on the following:

How does the programme begin?

Does it start with a soft-story or does it go straight into the news of the day?

Do they have a soft news segment? This segment is when they have a softer type of story, like a lotto win or a world record attempt. Would you have anything to offer along these lines?

Or is the show covering mainly hard news like courts, inquests, murders, business stories and international news?

How many interviews does the programme have? Are they a mix of hard (courts, politics) and soft (light-hearted)? Is there any trend that you can see regarding the type of interviews that are done?

Is there a particular day of the week that seems to have a softer focus – could it be Friday, for example, which is a popular day to devote to more light-hearted content. Viewers that follow a show know this and tune in knowing that Fridays are different.

Do they have guest slots? What kind of guests do they have? Do they have experts in?

Do they take viewers' questions? You are a business, but you are also a viewer – don't forget that.

Do they profile a business? I helped a client pitch for this type of slot on a national radio station, and he got coverage after we tailored his pitch. We both listened to this slot a few times, emailed and had some calls with each other about ideas and then sat down to write a pitch together. I knew what angles were most likely to be picked up. I needed to know if he was happy going outside of his comfort zone, and he was. He got a 20-minute slot for his business. This resulted in numerous follow-ups including a magazine shoot and lots of interest in his business.

What other types of slots are there? Money. Fashion. Pets. Food…the list goes on.

Do they have a social media slot? Some programmes post up funny photos from social media, or videos. Do they go through a Twitter feed or post up photos from Instagram? Is this something you can take a look at and take action on?

Do they have a lot of viewer interaction?

Do any of the presenters wear quirky clothes or like certain things, like shoes? Do any of them have a love of dogs? Is there something about any of the presenters that you could tap into?

Then ask, how do you fit in? You may listen to one show and know instantly that you wouldn't fit in. So, scratch it off your list and replace it with another. Then go through the process again.

Breakfast shows tend to focus on bringing viewers up to date with what has happened that morning or the evening before or overnight. They have up to the minute news stories that have happened from the evening/day before, right up to what is happening that day. If your story is a feature about a topic that has happened a long time ago, then this will not work. These types of shows are hugely dependent on the time factor. They are of the now, of the moment. But they are also peppered with more light-hearted items like fashion, health, beauty. If you don't fit into a set part of the news agenda, then you need to look and see how you can make yourself relevant to another area. Don't shoehorn yourself in, as a researcher will recognise that. Try to make yourself relevant. And the only way to find out where you fit is by (you said it) watching the show!

Targets and time

Set targets. Set realistic ones. Be realistic about what you can and can't do. Take two weeks to start with. Two weeks when you know you have time to dedicate to your research of broadcast outlets you want to learn more about. This will give you some perspective on whether you like this kind of work (because it is work) or if you need to outsource this to someone else. If you are serious about getting featured, you need to stick at it. **Don't ignore shows at the weekend**. This is because weekend shows are hugely popular, and some are way more popular than the weekday ones. Keep the process going for 14 days and I believe that you will start to have a clearer picture of what makes media outlets tick and what makes news. You will also be hundreds of steps ahead of those who don't bother to do this.

In 14 days, you should have a good knowledge of at least 2 television shows, 2 radio shows, and 4-5 newspapers or magazines. I know people who manage to achieve more than this, but if you hit this target, you have done very well. Take time to congratulate yourself for making this important step and for furthering your knowledge to get publicity.

What to do with this information

You have all this information, now what to do with it? I make this simple by using four columns. You can use Word or Excel, or a large A3 sheet on your wall. Whatever suits.

- In the first column, list out potential story ideas.
- In the second column, have the segments of shows or just shows that you feel may be worth sending your potential stories to.
- In the third, put who you are sending to and what the angle is.
- The fourth column should include the times of year that you

could potentially send one of your stories. Like I mentioned earlier, International Women's Day, Childhood Cancer Month, Black History Month, Valentine's Day, Christmas etc.

Make this file one you can share with your team, and make it accessible from anywhere. This ensure that it remains an active document and not one that sits on your desk or in your laptop and doesn't get used. Or make a copy of it and put it up in a place where everyone can see it and offer suggestions. It should be integral to each of your attempts to get publicity.

Getting all this information together in one place is hugely informative and rewarding. Start to join the dots together as to what stories could suit a particular outlet and a particular time of year. This makes your strategy more robust and cohesive as you will find opportunities to go after or create and you won't be tempted to blast out your release to everyone as this never works.

The one thing that is important in this exercise is to take notes that will make sense to you and your team in weeks or months from now. Always state why you think a certain segment is relevant to the business. Don't just write down that you liked it. Make a certain point about it. This is important as it will make more sense to have this information to use in your email to the show's researcher to show you are engaging with their content.

Always date your notes and where possible when you go to send your story, I would suggest referencing something relevant that you know happened in the show recently, if it applies. Or at least referencing something you like about the show, even if it isn't relevant to your pitch. It is important to show that you have been engaging.

Once you've pitched, don't stop listening to that show altogether. But plan your time wisely and go to the second show on your list and start listening to that before you pitch. This is the time-consuming part of this process, but it is one that will pay off in the long run, as you will have gained knowledge of what will or will not suit the show you are planning to pitch to. And the best thing about this is that you have this information for life; all you will need to do is update it once in a while (I recommend doing this twice a year). The longer you listen/watch shows, the more information you will be armed with when it comes to pitching your story.

Let's do lunch

The above generally apply to every show. However, lunchtime shows are slightly different. They normally come after the heavy news programmes, and so cater to a different audience. The lunchtime audience want a light talk show or music chat show. They want to get away from the hard news that has dominated the morning. So, some of their targets include stay at home parents, grandparents, people who are finished work early or at 3pm, people who are off work, unemployed, older age groups, and younger age groups. They are also targeting businesses and clients who might be visiting hairdressers, medical waiting rooms and beauty salons. There is a mixture of a lot of elements, but they tend to generally stay away from hard news unless it is a major story, and it would be remiss of them to not cover it.

You will find that these shows have become more targeted rather than trying to be a catch-all. There are lunchtime shows that are very much talk shows targeted primarily at women. Go watch *Loose Women,* a popular UK show, for example. Their audience is totally female orientated. They make no excuse for that and that is why it works well. Other lunchtime shows solely include more light-hearted segments, from music interviews to fashion, beauty, human interest stories, challenges, fun items, and seasonal segments They like to set out their agenda and stick to it. **Again, I repeat: your knowledge of the various shows and your possible place in them will only come by watching the shows numerous times and getting a feel for what fits.**

Having a late-night?

If you are working on a political campaign or an election, you are most likely interested in the evening or late-night shows, as they mostly concentrate on the topics of the day, political stories, hard news stories and high-profile court cases. This is the time when viewers are sitting on their couches and are ready to see expert commentators enlighten them about a pressing issue that happened that day or is about to happen. Oftentimes, evening shows are following up on stories that have made the headlines during the day. A story that broke that morning is still running into the evening.

Evening shows usually start late in the evening, like 9/10pm, so you need to keep this in mind if you are planning to target these shows. If you have something particularly controversial to say concerning the topic(s) of the day, these shows are ideal for you to pitch to. Having something controversial to say that you can stand over is newsworthy to these shows because they are always looking for someone who is going against the grain. If you are that type of person, you will need to be ready for some tough questions on your stance and be able to stand over your story. Make sure you are not jeopardising your business by pushing yourself too far out there. Only you can be the best judge of that.

But before you put time into pitching for evening shows ask yourself these questions:

- How are you going to get there if they want you to appear on the show? The show's studios could be a three-hour drive away. And they may want you there that evening or the following evening.

- Do you or your spokesperson have the time to do this type of show? Remember these shows will probably want their guests in by at least 6pm to get them ready, go through anything they will be discussing, do make-up and hair, and get to know the presenters and the run of the show. You will need to factor in this time to prepare for the show.

Evening shows can often be the most difficult for people. People are often attending by themselves, as other colleagues are at home watching it. So, if you have never been on a tv set before, it can be quite daunting. Before you go on, you will watch everything that happens on the other side of the camera. And you may be getting to hang out with other celebs, some of which you may be a huge fan of. It is hard not to get caught up in all the behind-the-scenes action. There are the huge lights, the set, getting make-up and hair touched up every few minutes, and getting treated like a special guest. It is okay to get caught up in all of this but remember why you are there and be ready for your moment when the cameras are on.

Repurposing your content

Yes, you can send the same release with the same basic information as a starting point. In fact, this is a major help when it comes to times of the year when you really need to ramp up your publicity. You have a starting point, and you can use the basis of this release and then tweak it for different times of the year that make it more relevant.

For example, Saving Tips for Back to School could be used every year but each time you would try to make it more relevant to that particular year or a particular funding scheme or an issue parents are facing in the lead up to this time. The same basics of a release, yes, but a different slant and some different content. However, I don't recommend using this for long periods as you will need to update everything to reflect trends and talking points.

Be a member of the audience

If it is a show that you want to get on, why not apply to be in the audience as a first step? There, you will get to see how the show works, the vibe of the show, how the audience reacts to certain items, what happens during the commercial breaks – everything! It is so worth it if you have the time to go to shows. And when you are ready to send your pitch to appear on the show, you can mention that you were previously in the audience, how you enjoyed it, what segments you liked, what you learned, and how you think you might fit in. This is a definite plus point when it comes to standing out.

The Irish television show *The Late Late Show* sends out calls for audience applications from time to time during the year. Chat shows in general are always open to applications. You could, if you wanted, let them know about you in your audience application. You could be plucked from the audience. I worked with two people who I advised to do this, and researchers asked them to be part of a segment on the show. It was a short appearance, but it gave them a taste of what it is like to be interviewed live. They both got business and further media attention from their short on-camera pieces. One got a major feature in a magazine while the other got interviewed on local radio about their appearance on the show.

If you have a seasonal product like a Christmas toy or other festive item, then you need to get a head start and start applying to be in the audience well in advance. At certain times of the year, there is more demand for audience tickets, so you need to be aware of that. Times like Christmas, Valentine's, and St Patrick's Day come to mind.

Always remember why you are there

You are there to tell a story. Your story. It is unique, and you want to make it as memorable for the audience as possible. You want viewers to remember you and want to know more about you and your story. I'm often surprised when people come off shows and are disappointed. Mainly because the presenters focused on something so minuscule or something that wasn't a major talking point from the company's point of view. My response is: You need to see this from the viewer's viewpoint. The presenters, researchers, producers know what their audience likes. They have the statistics to prove it. What is minuscule to you may be a big point to the listeners or viewers. You just didn't know it then.

Presenters are human too and they may have had an off-day or were not given enough information about you to do a good interview. Don't let this get you down. You got to be on the show, something most people dream of, and you got to talk about you and your business.

Steer the conversation back to your story - if you can

You may not get to talk about your expertise at all. If this happens, it is up to you to try to steer the conversation back to why you are there. This is not always easy, but you can try to start your sentences with: "When I was doing this…" or "I always look at this with the knowledge I got from …" Insert your expertise into these sentences. That way you can steer it back towards you, but not in an overly salesy way. Look at it this way. If you have done a decent job, then these viewers will go to your website and get all the other information there. So, don't be worried that viewers won't find you. And don't let your worry come across on camera. Go with the flow and trust that being there and getting the publicity will do your company a lot of good.

If the segment takes a more humorous turn, then go with it, trust that you will get something from this. If you do a good job and show that you can think on your feet, then you might even get a call back from the television show. Remember that shows find it difficult to get guests that are informative, good on camera, with a sense of humour, an ability to go with the flow and easy to deal with. If you have some of these traits, you will be remembered for future segments around your expertise.

Okay, so it goes wrong

Now, imagine you've sent someone onto a television show, or you are going on yourself. You've done a huge amount of preparation and you feel you are as ready as you can be. And you or your spokesperson don't nail it. It goes badly. In fact, it is a talking point in the office and online.

Firstly, don't blame yourself or the spokesperson you have assigned to do that interview (someone within your company, CEO, Product Manager etc). If it was a particularly bad mistake, then take the time to evaluate it and you may decide to release a statement about it to clarify anything that was incorrect. Or apologise if you feel the need to. Owning up to mistakes and providing an explanation is a better approach than burying your head in the sand. Take the time to watch the show back and go through areas that need improvement. Concentrate on getting better for the next appearance instead of wallowing in negativity.

I know one coach who did a terrible job on her first radio appearance. She phoned me after and cried down the phone. She picked herself back up and the next time she appeared on that same radio show, she referenced her first appearance as a joke. She had learned from what she had done wrong and wasn't afraid to admit it. By referencing her mistakes, her followers could see that she was human, that she messes up just like them, but she was getting back in the race and back on a radio show to do it all again. The presenters also appreciated that, and they were on her side, hoping she'd redeem herself. The second time, she was much better. And she got asked back a third time!

Don't concentrate on regurgitating information

Oftentimes, things don't go well mainly because you or your spokesperson didn't go with the flow. All the information is in your or their heads and they are trying desperately to remember it all. With the lights, heat, and nerves, it is difficult to forget that you need to relax. Also, you can request that the presenters mention your website at the end of the interview or put it on screen as your name is introduced to viewers. So, if you have strayed off topic or gotten nervous, they can wrap up the segment by giving your information and putting it up on the screen and also on their website. Remember to ask about this when you are talking to researchers about your guest appearance.

Online buzz about your appearance

Have someone back at base posting online and creating some online excitement about the show. Get the spokesperson to send or post up photos of themselves backstage or with the presenters, arriving at the show, photos of the set, or ones with other guests. Or if he/she is more comfortable get them to send this information to someone on the team to post up for them. Make it easy for them. Have someone by their email to do the posting and to come up with fun captions. Being on a show is a lot of pressure and teamwork at a time like this helps. If you don't have a team, then hiring someone for just a few hours like a virtual assistant could really help. Reach out to people in your community for help. You can offer to do the same for them if they get on a show.

Remember to tag the show in the photos. This is another way of building up excitement. Also, have other employees share them too. It is in everyone's best interests to be online for a short period and then they can get back to their evening. Also, it is important that you have someone watching in case something needs to be followed up on urgently. This is rare but it does happen when stories break or when a presenter or someone in the audience asks a question that needs further clarification.

Oh, and do I really need to say this?...Don't have any alcohol beforehand! As tempting as this might be, just to calm those nerves a little, don't do it. Have a celebratory drink afterwards with the other guests. Always remember to have water with you and to have eaten before you get there. Don't rely on both of these things being there for you because they may not be.

A quick summary:

Morning: People are eating breakfast and want to catch up with what has happened in the world overnight or what is about to happen.

Afternoon: People are taking a time out, looking for something a little less taxing, something funny, good-natured, uplifting.

Evening: So, what has happened today? Has anything major occurred in the world that people need to hear about or reflect on? What were the election results? Who is the new US President? Stories from the morning can still be making major news headlines in the evening.

Some reminders:

Watch and listen to the shows. There is no better way to learn where you fit in. Tailor your release to a show's segment. Demonstrate your knowledge of the show in your pitch. Be prepared. If this involves getting coaching for your spokesperson, then do it. There is nothing more damaging than getting a slot on a tv show and for your spokesperson to not be prepared and ready. Remember this is a show. It is not going to be all about you and your product/service. The presenters have to think of the listeners/viewers. They may focus entirely on one aspect of what you sent in if they see this as the most interesting piece of information. Be prepared to not get all your information out there. Be ready for the phone to ring afterwards.

Be ready to capitalise

If it is a product, have it in stock. If it's available on your website, then have it on the home page. Try to have a discount or some offer when people arrive. You can link it into the show by using a hashtag with the show's name. For example, get them to use the coupon code #latelateshowoffer.

Make sure that other employees know about the show. Get them to tweet or Facebook their friends about. Get them to spread the word and share the show's content. Remember, shows need content, but they also get a lot of submissions. Help yourself stand out by being relevant.

I've been on morning, afternoon, and evening shows. One good practical tip is to drink water and brush your teeth beforehand (bring a toothbrush and toothpaste with you). I have seen people who were unable to speak due to a dry mouth and those who made headlines for having food stuck in their teeth. And that was the only talking point afterwards! Also, if you have to leave the set for any reason, let a member of the team know. You don't want them panicking just because you popped outside for a short walk to clear your head. They will need to know where you are all the time so be courteous and let them know.

Publicity Exercise

Tell yourself this: I will educate myself on my chosen broadcast outlets because I know this is one of the best ways to get publicity.

Then, answer the following:

What media outlets am I going to learn about (list at least 3)?

What time in my day am I going to devote to this? Morning, afternoon, or evening?

What segments most interest me, and why?

CHAPTER 9

SUPPLEMENTS – THE UNTAPPED GEM OF PUBLICITY

Before I sat down to write this chapter, I spent some time looking through the supplements I worked on during my time as a journalist. I read over past feature stories on ordinary people doing amazing things, people and their businesses, helpful guides, uplifting stories, and a travel guide to the south of France, written by someone who lived there. I got lost in the world of escapism and entertainment that supplements offer readers and it reminded me of how passionate I am about them.

Supplements are an excellent way of getting publicity yet are hugely underutilised by many looking to get featured. They are one of my biggest passions when it comes to getting publicity and I always urge clients to create a strategy to target supplements in their niche every year. I get my clients to learn about the supplements that are printed/published online in their area and pitch to them at least 3-4 times a year. People get so consumed by wanting to get featured in the main paper that they forget that getting featured in a supplement based on their area of expertise is exactly where they need to be. Supplements are so often overlooked because businesses feel that readers don't pay much attention to them. The fact is that the opposite is true. Supplements are a key way to focus on one thing that grabs the attention of those who are experts in that area and those who want/need to learn more about this topic.

Readers love supplements

Let me explain. A supplement that is inserted into a Saturday or Sunday newspaper or is a weekday special has elements of interest to the reader that last the whole week – feature stories, tv guide, crossword, recipes, tips, book listings, and so on. It will be opened more times than the regular newspaper. This supplement sits on a coffee table for a whole week and sometimes even longer and is most likely used by everyone in the house. Or at least looked at. Some people buy a Saturday or Sunday newspaper based on the supplement. They want to see a celebrity on the front or a person's story they can relate to. They want to feel like the supplement is a bonus that they will get something from. A good feature story pulls them in.

If you get placed in a supplement targeted to your ideal reader, for example, a supplement about weddings, pregnancy, exercise, high blood pressure, healthy eating, summer breaks or winter breaks, then you are most likely going to have ideal readers reading your story. And the newspapers who print these at certain times of the year know when their readers expect such content. They have in most cases tried and tested it many times. So, in essence the newspaper is doing a lot of the hard work here by already offering you the chance to get featured at a time that they know readers want to read about such content.

Wedding supplements are huge business. People getting married need information about everything to do with their wedding. The list of items needed is endless. I know a hat designer that bases her business publicity entirely around wedding supplements, saying it is the best time for her to leverage media publicity. She never expressed an interest in seeking publicity in the main section of a newspaper. Most importantly, she didn't need to.

Newspapers and magazines promote their supplements in a major way. In issues leading up to the publication of the supplement, media outlets will promote the supplement on the front page of an issue and on their site's homepage. They will often tease a story to get their readers interested ahead of time. If it is an exclusive interview with a well-known actor or writer or a royal, these are often promoted weeks in advance.

A lot of time and effort goes into making a good supplement. Stories need to be researched, good photos are essential, so too is a good layout. I would argue that customers reading a supplement value layout more than anything. It makes the supplement easier to read and this helps make it feel different from the newspaper. You will need to have good photos to stand a chance at featuring.

Supplements about holidays are also huge. I remember one I worked on that focused on holidays in the west of Ireland with a focus on the Wild Atlantic Way and we ended up printing a second run of it as B&B's, hostels, pubs, restaurants, and all types of tourist outlets wanted copies to share with visitors. The people who were featured received huge publicity and customers came knocking.

Supplements around a special anniversary, an event coming up, or an annual festival in your area are ones you should look at next time they are printed by your local or national newspaper. Readers are particularly drawn to these supplements because they expect to see people that they know in them. The newspaper is expected to go all out in their efforts to focus on an annual event. A newspaper I worked in did a 48-page supplement on a fishing festival every year because it was a major event in the town and readers wanted all the information in one place along with stories, a calendar of events, and photos. Also, the newspaper has a huge increase in sales during this week's publication purely because of the supplement.

Plan your media strategy around supplements

Okay, you are probably thinking there is a lot of studying to be done! And you're right. There is. But once you narrow down what you want to do, all you have to do after that is top it up. You could follow my earlier example about a hat designer and just focus on supplements alone. To plan a media strategy around supplements, this is what I think you need to do to give yourself a chance at success.

- Keep a copy of a previous supplement that targets your ideal customer, i.e., weddings, music, health, fitness. Study it and start to figure out how you can fit in.

- Look at the supplements in your local and regional area and start marking in your calendar the likely times they are run.

- **Ask these newspapers for their supplement list**. Here you will see the times of the year they do their supplements, and you will get to know when you should be pitching to them. By having this list, you will start to see a pattern and from there you can plan a media strategy around these times. You'll also get a sense of what timeframe you need to work to so you can have your content ready. For example, if you are planning to pitch to a summer wedding supplement, you will most likely be starting to get your pitch together by Feb/March and pitching it that month for a wedding supplement that would be coming out in April/May in time to help brides during the upcoming summer.

Ask about the deadline

Also, don't take March as the deadline, do your research on the outlets you want to get featured in and map out a strategy by working backward at least two months from the date of publication. For major publications, work back at least 4 months and give yourself longer if you can.

The best way to be certain though is to ask. This is also a good way to start a conversation with a media outlet by showing interest in a future publication that they are most likely planning and working on alongside their day-to-day activities. Also, note that brides get ready years in advance. People book holidays well in advance. So, plan out a strategy that continually gets you featured so you get in front of your ideal audience regularly. Think of this as a way to get customers well into the future. You may not see a return on this straightaway. But you are increasing your visibility and getting into their minds.

Think of supplements as a way to build your following, your email list, and your customer base. Also, look at supplements as a way of getting customers at other times of the year not just around the time of summer weddings if we take that as an example. There will be brides and grooms reading your content that will be getting married at Christmas or New Year and could be looking for you. (Of course, I am using a wedding supplement as an example, but this applies to all supplements).

Value to readers

If you haven't guessed by now, I love supplements and I loved working on them. What I enjoyed most was seeing them come together and picturing the reader getting as much value as possible from them. I know readers who buy newspapers specifically for the supplement. Supplements have in-depth feature pieces, are very niched down, have reviews of products/books/movies, look pretty, often have offers of some kind and giveaways, and a television guide at the back. What's not to like!

However, they are expensive to produce and many need to be able to fund themselves through advertising. And while the advertising is important, getting readers to buy will only happen if the content offers value. Keep this in the forefront of your mind when you pitch to supplement editors. Your story must be of value to readers. It must solve a problem, prevent them from having a problem or provide a map showing them exactly what they need to do to have success.

How you can get value

The pre-planning, planning and strategy that go into a supplement is huge. If a supplement has been done before in the same area and many outlets will have done numerous wedding supplements, say for example, then the supplement team will pick two to three of their past issues by way of research. They will evaluate what worked, looked well and what didn't. When it comes to doing another wedding supplement, they will do some analysis of what stories did well, who sent in good photos, who was easy to deal with and met deadlines. You may think that journalists and advertising executives don't remember such details because things are so fast paced, but they do. They will base some of their content around knowing who to contact that is reliable and professional.

Supplements are planned weeks or months in advance, so

businesses offering anything within the area focused on in the supplement are contacted by sales executives to see if they are interested in paying for an advert. Certain places within the supplement (front and back pages, pages 3, 5, 7, and middle pages) are the most expensive. You should check this with each outlet though in case they have different guidelines.

So, if you do decide to take out an advert, you need to make sure you get good value in both your advert and in any editorial that you send in. These two are not inextricably linked but I am finding that more so these days they are starting to become inseparable in some outlets, particularly trade publications and some local ones. Be ready to be asked if you have a budget for advertising.

Supplements are only as good as the stories inside

For the content side of things, it is the best on offer at that particular time that is chosen by the journalists and editors. However, major advertisers will use their bargaining power to get large features inside. But these features will have to be story-driven and not salesy. A supplement will only survive if it has good stories, first and foremost. If there is an agreement in place to have an editorial included based on the purchase of an advert, you may find that the journalist may be assigned to interview you if your sent-in content isn't good enough. Which is a win for you. You will be getting a professionally written story about you to back up your advert. Even if your advert is a small one compared to the larger businesses, I encourage you to exert your power here especially if this has been communicated to you in any emails received by the publication. Things do get missed between advertising and editorial so make sure you are clear in what content you want to be considered for inclusion. Don't assume that your content will get included. Follow up on this.

You are the one spending money, so you should be ready with a press release in hand to send in once you agree to be part of a supplement. You should push your content and re-emphasise its value. Your influence will vary greatly depending on the kind of outlet you are working with. The bigger the outlet, the harder it is to get your content featured. Your content has to be amazing. Let's be clear, you do have some leverage when it comes to getting your copy featured but don't push it. It may just not be included this time but next time it could be. There are a lot of moving parts when it comes to putting a supplement together so it may have to be left out for a number of reasons.

Also, know that there are newspapers who siphon off sections of a supplement to satisfy major advertisers and they will have an agreement in place to put their content in there. Major advertisers will have huge marketing budgets and their content will add value, have a story, and fit the subject matter of the supplement. They will also be key to the media outlet breaking even on a supplement or making a profit. Having key advertisers in there looks well for everyone as they will help to drawn in more readers. They may also offer a large giveaway which will also entice more readers in. Which means more people will get to see your content as well.

The bigger the names that are in there, the more enticing it looks to readers. Remember that even though these major advertisers will be taking space, there are plenty of other opportunities. You just need to position yourself in such a way that your story can also find a home in the supplement.

Don't repeat your advert copy verbatim in your story content

If you do advertise, remember that your advert is for your sale. Don't go repeating that verbatim in your story content. But do try to link them if you can. For example, if you have a person in your advert, you could use that same person in the photo alongside your story. But have them doing something different. Use different photos with the same person.

If you have a promotion, you will feature that in your advert, but you can also insert that into your story content. Have the links obvious enough so that a casual reader equates the two as being from the same company. Offering different things in both helps you to appeal to a reader who may not look at adverts and vice versa. The readers who love to see good deals will go to read your story for more details.

Let's go into more detail on this because when I've seen this work, it can really catapult a business's visibility. Okay, the content or your press release should have something different. Get a customer story, a transformational story that takes the reader on a journey, use your own personal story. It must be newsworthy to be considered and to make it in, especially in bigger publications.

Your advert can offer a discount. You can ask that this be highlighted as an inclusion on the supplement's front page, especially if it is something worthy of a reader's attention.

You can ask a question in the story/press release that only has the answer to it in the advert or vice versa, literally getting the reader to look at both. Do yourself a major favour and not have identical copy in both advert and story. This also places you higher up the list of getting featured than those that do the same thing in both.

So how do you make the most of getting your copy featured?

Like I said above, you can try to use the same person in both your advert and story. Also, use the same colour scheme. Use the same tagline that you have in your advert in your press release/story copy. It might not get used as is, but the journalist will know what you are trying to do and may be willing to go along with it. Remember, journalists want the best supplement that is possible within the timeframe allowed.

Tailor your story to the supplement's theme. Get in touch with the journalist to see how best you can do this. They will thank you for asking. Don't be tempted to send a generic piece of content that you could send to any supplement. Your copy needs to be relevant and not a piece you have sent out to numerous outlets with a general overview of what you do. Go back, edit it, and make it fit the supplement's subject matter. You will be competing with many others for copy space. Keep this in mind and let it help drive you towards creating the best copy you can.

You have already been contacted by the advertising department to spend money, so you have a connection and a relationship to build on. Nurture this relationship and work on the content you want to get considered based on some feedback you receive. If you find you are not getting a response from the journalist, then don't be shy to ask if the salesperson knows of any particular types of content that are being sought after and offer to try to help.

The editor may have sent out an email requesting that copy be focused on a certain area this time. Oftentimes, when a supplement is done year on year, it is easy to resort to the same topics and sometimes these topics remain relevant. But an editor will know that readers will soon get turned off if they keep seeing the same things. Ask about particular angles that are needed. Then, target your content based on any insights you get. Have an angle. Don't be too general here. The best articles in supplements are ones that take an interesting angle on the subject matter. **You should treat the content for a supplement with the same importance as the way you treat it as if you were sending it into the regular newspaper**. I can't stress this enough. Some businesses look at supplements differently, like readers don't pay as much attention to them as they would to the regular newspaper. This is a wrong assumption and something you need to become aware of. Readers love good supplements. Good supplements have a lot to offer. Remember, a good supplement sits on someone's coffee table for a week or more. Some are kept for life.

It is amazing to consider that you have the chance to be seen numerous times by numerous people in one house. A supplement doesn't have an exact date for when it has expired. This is up to the reader to decide. A newspaper's issue is different; it is for that particular day or week. Okay, so the television guide will be out of date in a week but there are feature stories, articles, how-to pieces, health tips, personal insights, recipes, puzzles, exercise articles, and workouts that link to videos on the web and so much more that encourage the reader to keep a supplement for longer.

Stakeholders and future relationships

You will be part of a polished pull-out or supplement and this is something you can show stakeholders, investors, and customers too. If you are building a collaboration or forging new relationships, then they also become a great way to show how serious you are about growing your visibility.

I encourage businesses to use any supplements that they have been featured in as a way of pitching for new business. Start putting the logos of any places you've been published up on your site and in all your company material. **Popular supplements** are Back to School, Health and Fitness, Alternative Medicine, Home and Garden, Home Building, Savings, Property, Christmas, Summer Holidays, Autumn Getaways, Valentine's Day, and Weddings. The latter is a huge money-maker.

What does a good supplement look like?

Like everything in life, some do things well and others fall a little short. This is the same in supplements. Some are pull-outs (what we call separate to the main section), others are stapled into the main section but have a front and back cover. Some are mid-week supplements; others are an integral part of a newspaper's offering at the weekend. So how do you spot a good supplement and one you would like to be featured in?

Some things to look out for are:

Good content with some of it written by reporters and others submitted by the marketing departments of businesses and other outside contributors/experts in the field.

Reader experiences. A personal story that relates to the topic of the supplement. The best reader experiences are ones written by the reader and edited by a journalist or editor to make them fit either with space in mind or with the subject matter in mind.

Photographs that are allowed room to breathe. Good photographs print well on glossy paper and supplements tend to use a different type of paper than that used by the main newspaper. This is to make it stand out and feel different when the reader picks it up. The supplement has a glossy texture to make the reader feel like there is high-value content inside. Online supplements apply the same idea by giving really good photos room to be appreciated on the page.

Good advertising. A well-told and put together advert is an important element of a good supplement. Supplement readers tend to see it all as one package and don't tend to strictly separate the advertising from the rest. This is mostly due to the presentation and layout of the supplement. When it's done well, the adverts are also there telling their story. It also shows that the advertising executives working on the advert copy want the readers to have an experience. The adverts are there to be of value to readers. It shows that everyone is invested in providing a good supplement.

Offers from advertisers and contributors. You can have the offer in your advert and in your copy. A good offer is a great way of getting featured in a supplement. Can you think of a good offer for a reader that you could offer? This is something that you can put into your pitch and a really good one can bolster your chances of getting included both inside and on the cover.

Helpful articles. Does the content help its ideal reader? Can your advert or story copy help readers? Do you have research you can share? Do you have top 10 tips on a topic or a top five things not to do? These types of articles break up the flow of content in supplements. They offer quick wins to the readers.

White space. A good supplement allows its content to breathe. It shouldn't look like everything is lying on top of each other and fighting for space. It is in the newspaper's best interests to make sure the supplement looks its best and everyone is happy. This might mean going up a few pages to allow for the content to not look crowded. Sometimes, too, it involves coming down a few pages to make up for cancellations. You won't necessarily know this but when you are involved in a supplement and are going over and back, an advertising executive may ask you if you want to increase your advert size or an editor might ask if you have more photos, depending on how the whole layout is going and how the jigsaw is being put together. Expect some over and back emails regarding your content.

A good front-page photo and headline. This is the most important page of the supplement. How does it look to you? What attracted you to this particular supplement? Take note of it. Don't think that your content isn't good enough for the front page. Always consider this an option open to you. Ask yourself what your headline is? Is it catchy? Is the photo good enough to carry a front page? (You will have followed my earlier advice and looked at previous supplements). If it is, don't be afraid to state this in your pitch, however, don't state it like you think it is a clear front runner. Just state that you feel it could be an option. The journalist receiving your email will be asked by the supplement's editor if they have any contenders for the front-page photo. Yours could well be on the list at the next meeting about the supplement. And by highlighting that you think you have an option worth considering, you are increasing your chances of having your email opened by the journalist. This is because you know that the journalist needs to have some photo options as he/she will be asked about this in the next meeting about the supplement.

Readers get a lot from these supplements. I'm highlighting this again because I've received so much feedback from readers who got inspired by articles, who wrote letters to me saying how much they enjoyed certain articles. We would also get letters from people who would tell us what they would like to see in the next supplement or things they felt could have been done better. Readers are engaged and they want stories they can connect with just like journalists want the same thing.

Do your research

Your first mission if you want to feature in a supplement is to do your homework. Look at supplements in your local and national press and get familiar with them right now. Look at what works, what interests you, what inspires you. Write it down and let this guide you towards your pitch development. I hope you start to see the value of supplements. They represent a massive way to reach the right audience and to showcase you and your business to people who are actively looking for what you do. Supplements targeted to your area of expertise means you are putting yourself in the best position to be seen by your ideal audience.

CHAPTER 10

THE CLASSIFIED ADVERTS: MORE THAN JUST A LONELY-HEARTS COLUMN

Why you should consider the classifieds section. YES! those small adverts at the back of your newspaper!

In my early days as a journalist, I was advised that I needed to read the newspaper I worked on from cover to cover. That meant everything and I was tested on it during my early weeks in my first newspaper job. Questions I got asked were what was the lead story in the Property Section? Who won the week's biggest game in the Sports Section? Who was this week's profiled businessperson? And near the end of this quiz, I'd get asked if I saw anything interesting in the Classifieds. Every week, I would look at this section, and I found stories in there that others wouldn't take the time to find. I didn't have to continue looking at the Classifieds once these first weeks of my induction transpired. This exercise was purely to get me to see and engage with everything in the publication. Most importantly, to be aware of publication in its entirety, not just the sections I wrote for. Looking back, it was an integral way to learn about what my colleagues did.

After this time, I decided to continue looking in the Classifieds because it was a source of the unexpected and as a journalist being surprised remains a great thrill. In those first weeks and throughout my years in newsrooms, I got some great gems of stories from simple classified adverts.

What are the Classifieds?

There may be some of you reading this and asking what is a classified and where do I find them?

The section: The classifieds section is where you find all the small adverts for cars, apartments, lessons in music, people looking for companions and so on. Some have photos, some don't. In fact, a photo doesn't necessarily need to be included. They are short and get to the point and often include a call to action and contact details.

It is in these small text adverts (they look like text boxes) that I found three of my best feature pieces as a young journalist. One man was selling the contents of his attic and was having an open sale. He invited people into his attic for a "viewing." He lit the steps up to his attic with some Christmas fairy lights and had some tea and cake for afterwards! A woman was selling her never worn wedding dress and was happy to talk about deciding not to get married which sparked a huge conversation among readers. Would you buy a wedding dress that was designed for the big day but never worn? Are you superstitious about these things?

Another story was from an elderly man who was setting up a group for men who had lost their partners and had no social outing. He wanted to hold the meetings at the local graveyard because most of the men he had spoken to visit the cemetery often.

All of these stories got major attention in other publications too. All this began with just a small advert that is well within the budget of most.

You may be able to help someone in a Classified Advert

As a short side note and putting publicity to one side for a moment, the classifieds are a great way to find anything you may be looking for, from a car to a holiday rental. You may also find props for a photoshoot (from an attic clear out). Remember, it is a place to put a small advert for your service and product. It is also a good place to find collaborations and also to find someone who you might be able to help.

And this brings me to my next point. **If you can help someone who has reached out in a Classified Advert, you have the start of a great story that you can pitch to the outlet that printed the advert.** It is a good way to generate story ideas for your business that you may not have ever thought of or considered.

Journalists do look here and the person in charge of laying out these pages sometimes lets a journalist know if they've read an interesting or unusual one that has come in. I'm always interested in the personal stories behind things people are selling, the problems people have and are trying to solve. So too are readers. There is always a story in there. Placing an interesting advert in this section can surprisingly get a lot of attention. But you'll need to concentrate on making it stand out. I've got some tips on how to do that.

Nothing is off the table

These small adverts at the back of a publication are where people sell small items, classes, property, cars, wedding services, musical instruments, and a host of other things. You will find also that property management companies and car companies are now using this space. So, nothing is off the table. In fact, people who look here including journalists are hoping to see something different or quirky.

You write the text from scratch. This includes the headline, the body of the text and your call to action. The advert is based pretty much entirely on text. The cost is based on the amount of words. You can add a photo, but these are small adverts by nature and photos don't always need to be present.

A good testing ground for an idea

It's about the story. You can write the story about a car you are trying to sell in a short number of words and get attention from qualified readers who are looking at this section to get a car. You don't get to rely on any aids like colour or design elements. This is about the text only. The text will be proofread by a sub-editor once you submit it and they might make some changes, but those changes will need to be cleared by you before final publication. If there is a problem with it, you will get notified and be asked to hold off until you fix an issue with the content.

These adverts are a way to stand out through your words only in a way that is much cheaper than a larger scale advert. This is a good place to test some content about a new product or service you plan to offer. You can use this as the first place to tell a snapshot of your story or to test a piece of copy and see if you get any responses.

The first ten words

If you can make the first 10 words of your advert really stand out, then you will have a better chance of getting attention. Think of the start of your small advert like you would the subject line of your email to a journalist. Some journalists look at this section for stories and trainees and interns most certainly look here and make a list of anything that interests them. They are at the start of their career and need to generate a storylist. I was that trainee many years ago. I loved reading the section and still do sometimes as people put their personality into their advert.

There are oftentimes at least one to two stories worth doing from this section. And the best thing is that a journalist has some good details to go on. Something has attracted this journalist to this advert. And there is a contact number to phone. Sometimes, longer press releases of 500+ words don't have any personality or a contact number! So, take a look at this section next time you look at a newspaper or magazine. See what others are doing in that space and test out some copy. Don't give up after a first attempt. Track its clicks (it will be online as well as on hard copy), refine and try again.

CHAPTER 11

WHY YOU DON'T HEAR BACK

You've sent it, you never hear back – What happened? For me, this is possibly the most asked question I get. Many people come to me incredibly frustrated because they did not get any response. They don't even know if the journalist opened it, if they read it or if it went straight to spam. Some journalists do have spam filters on for certain words and it can be hard to know which ones they would most likely have flagged. Which is why I always encourage you to not put "Press Release" in the subject line because during busy times journalists may turn on email filters and one that they might likely flag is "Press Release".

I've heard the story many times. You felt it was a good story, sent the pitch email or press release in, waited a few days before emailing again and are now thinking of phoning that journalist. You feel it is worthy of getting featured and now are losing hope and confidence. Some let this rejection get them down a lot and I can understand this especially if you really need the publicity. Some feel like they are doing something wrong in their business if a journalist doesn't validate them by doing an article. Sound familiar?

I want this chapter to be a place where you can come to when you are not getting a response and need some enlightenment and reminders about why this might be so. Open this chapter and see if there is something you are missing.

Firstly, I hope by now you have grasped that a newspaper/radio station/ television station has many busy elements to it. So often, people don't seem to understand that. Understanding that a journalist has a lot of hats to wear, and your story isn't the only one they are working on, is important and understanding this puts you ahead of most people who send in their release or pitch and expect coverage.

It also helps to take rejection as just another rejection and get ready to pick yourself back up and try again with another story. Some people feel they should still get featured even if a major event has just happened like a court case has taken a dramatic turn, a bomb has gone off or a child has just gone missing. They have no idea that a journalist has other stories to cover, and your pitch will fall off the list if anything major happens. Check in with the news cycle and see if the news reporters in your area or in your country have been reporting on a major event.

Media outlets in one week/one day could have all of these elements and more. Go look and see if they had any of the following:

- A major court case(s)
- A major celebrity photoshoot
- The death of a prominent figure
- Huge sports matches for the local or national side
- A feature on an issue or a person or a business
- A supplement in areas such as Health, Beauty, Lifestyle, Property, Business, or a Social Scene section

- An extended news section - Some news pages dedicated to an event or breaking story
- The sports pages (as well as the huge matches)
- More advertising than normal – sourcing, getting copy, design, review of design, sign-off, and print (this is reiterated hundreds of times)
- Major advertising features and more full-page adverts than usual or more advertorials
- A wrap around front page (one that stretches across the front and back cover)
- A blacked-out cover – if a major event happened where many people died or if a popular person in the city/town passed away
- Natural disasters – flooding or a heatwave – these stories take over publications when they happen because readers need updates
- And a front and back cover that is more detailed than normal – these two pages are what journalists and editors are constantly thinking about every day at work and oftentimes at home too.

Journalism is not a 9-5 job. And this for daily newspapers is their daily schedule. For weeklies, this is a weekly schedule. The machine never stops. Journalists and editors are always thinking about how they need to respond to events and what is the most appropriate response. This requires a lot of thought, research and making calls to assess how to respond.

Because journalists are so busy, this offers both opportunities as well as downsides like when a journalist has too much on their plate in a given week to deal with your story. You send in your pitch amid all this activity that is already going on. It is difficult to stand out. That is where building relationships, having perseverance and persistence are your greatest assets.

Are you in the now? And are you ready?

Radio and television always work in the now. If you are sending to them, you need to be reacting to something that is happening now or is about to happen. You also need to be ready to react if they want to cover your story. Not next week or not when your website is up and running or when your schedule is a little lighter. Now on television or radio now is literally right now. They work on the same stories listed above but they need the information for their next broadcast which is in the next hour.

If you are pitching to them and they phone you and you don't pick up that first time, you've missed your chance. If your story is an exceptional one, then you may get another phone call. And if you don't pick up on the second try, you've definitely missed your chance. Check your phone. Have you got a missed call from a number you don't know? This is a simple one, but it can often be the reason. You simply missed the boat.

Think sections – did you pitch to a person or any specific section?

Think of the media outlet you are looking at in terms of people and the sections they write for. Think of journalists as people who are trying to write their best story. I go into this in more detail in another chapter about how a newspaper is put together. For now, if you are pitching something for Health, Beauty, Lifestyle, Empowerment anything that is lifestyle-related, then these sections are done well in advance. If you are pitching to a section and your deadline is imminent, you will have most likely not given yourself enough time to get featured.

Are you aware of the news agenda?

Let me give you some insights into what happens when a major story breaks. There has been a shooting or a terrorist attack and a member of the public, a source or a relative of one of the journalist's phones in to say, "Have you heard that this happened?" The already busy newsroom turns into a chaotic scene where an editor pulls together 2-3 journalists for a meeting and assigns jobs just like that. They don't get to finish what they've been doing (they may probably do this as they wait for information on the major story, but they simply just may not have time).

Their minds now turn to the main story of the day. The pressure is immense. The clock is ticking and all of a sudden, a journalist has to write 800 to 1,000 words on a breaking story that he/she may only have the bare details of and now needs to get answers to lots of questions from people who will be hard to get hold of or don't want to talk. They need to have good sources at times like this. As well as getting the main story, they will need others to weigh in on it as well like any experts or people that are good for reactions/comments (often politicians, mayors, businesspeople, lecturers).

A radio or television reporter needs to get to the scene or interview someone who was there, so they have something to broadcast while they wait for information from the police. It is pressure like no other. And add to this the pressure to get accurate details. And add to this the pressure to tell it in a way that makes sense, and that readers and listeners will understand. Lots of calls need to be made to clarify information that was gotten in earlier calls. It needs to be a balanced article.

The people that need to be called may not understand or care that the journalist has a deadline. They may need to ask their boss who may need to ask their boss if they can speak with the journalist. Details are sketchy on every level and a story cannot run unless the details are accurate. Photos or footage are needed from the scene (if it's a crime) or of the person that has died or done something that has shocked/saddened or surprised everyone like a shock resignation for example.

Often in a matter of hours, journalists from local, national, and international media descend on this one story. National and international journalists will seek out local reporters for local knowledge and for who to interview. They are on a deadline too. Remember reporters help each other at times like this. Unless one of them has an exclusive, then it remains an exclusive until they are ready to release it.

AND you just happen to send in your press release about a new product launch or an open day. Something which in fairness is huge news to you, you've worked on it for a long time, and you are now ready to grab some limelight for it. You hit send. Never hear anything about it ever again. It is because you couldn't have picked a worse time to send it in. It is hard to predict this of course but knowing that this could have been the reason puts your mind at rest. And it helps you get back up and pitch it again because you'll have given yourself plenty of time to have another go at it.

Timing

When you send in your release/photo/pitch in to a journalist says a lot about you and your business. If you have sent it in on the same day as a major news story is breaking, it is difficult for you to stand out. In fairness, you may just have timed it wrong but if the story has broken and is making international headlines and you send in your release, it shows you have no regard for the news of the day. If you send your release in on deadline day, it shows that you have no clue about the newspaper's schedule. Deadline day is the most stressful and it is when space is at a premium. Journalists are waiting on loads of other emails to come in that are connected with stories they need to get done now. Sending in a release about a product that can be printed at any time, shows you haven't done your homework. Your email will get lost and most likely won't be opened.

All the other reasons you didn't make it this time

- You sent it to the wrong person. That person no longer works there.

- You sent it to the right person but have addressed them by the name of someone working in another newspaper or publication (this has happened to me plenty of times). It shows you are blanket emailing this release in the hope that someone will pick it up.

- You sent it to the editor on deadline day and it is buried in thousands of emails.

- You sent it to info@thenewspaper.com and it got buried in an email account that an intern gets to work through. An intern who might be there or might not be.

- Your press release is badly written. It doesn't have an interesting headline. It doesn't have any quotes.

- Or your quotes are long and don't say much. Use your quotes wisely. Don't let them run on and on.

- Your press release is a summary. There is no story.

- It is not immediate. There is no urgency. Ask: why should a journalist do this story now? Get some urgency into your copy.

- Your story isn't relevant to what is going on in this area right now.

- Your photos are from your Facebook page. These do not print well.

- Your photos are links that don't work. Sometimes, there is no meat.

- There is no story. No story = no publication.

- Sometimes, there is too much information yet there is no angle or hook. The journalist doesn't know where to begin.

- Your release/pitch is old. You missed the boat by not sending in your release when the issue was timely. If you have an angle on a breaking or running story, you need to decide there and then whether you want to be a part of it. You can't wait. You need to decide and either let it go or go for it. Remember there will be other times but trust your gut feeling. Sometimes a better opportunity to get huge coverage may not come along again for a while, if ever.

How not to annoy journalists

Okay, so this list details things that stop you from getting coverage.

In fairness, you are doing these things without the knowledge that they are not going to work. And journalists are aware that not everyone knows how to approach a media outlet for publicity. You also don't want to annoy a journalist. Having said that, journalists are used to be being annoyed, it generally comes with the territory. So, when you don't annoy them, you stand out. Trust me, I always remember those whose method of contacting me was just so brilliant, I wanted to thank them. And oftentimes, I did send a thank you email back to let them know. Just keep this in mind as you go on this journey. Don't pester them by calling regularly asking about your press release, don't stalk or tag them on social media asking why they haven't got back to you.

Exceptions

Having said that, there are exceptions to this when urgently contacting journalists is merited. But tread carefully! If you have a story that you feel merits getting featured like you've sold a EuroMillions ticket, you've won a million (if you feel like sharing that), you've just seen a helicopter crash in your back yard, then yes, by all means, contact the paper/radio/television show but this is best done by phone. Others include your business has just been nominated for a prestigious award like an Oscar or Emmy, or it has won a major award in business or just been endorsed by a major Hollywood celebrity. This merits a phone call to the news desk with urgency in your pitch.

In times like this, speaking to a reporter is best but be prepared for all the questions you will get asked. Many people that have called me over the years didn't have all the information clear in their heads. It happens a lot. This could be basic stuff like addresses or names of places. And its fine, ordinary people don't think like journalists. But it's important to have some of the basic information – the who, what, where, when, and how parts. Are you willing for your photo to be taken? Another vital question to have an answer to. You don't want to regret having your photo taken say if you've won the lottery.

Ask the journalist (Or ask the media outlet's receptionist)

What if you can't figure out exactly when the best time is to send something in? Why not send an email to the reporter you are targeting and ask them when it is best to send in your material? I'm amazed at how many people don't do this. Why not? It's a way of introducing yourself and you've also thought about the schedule of the journalist and being mindful of what works best. Use the email to introduce yourself and what you do. Then send your story in at the time they ask you to.

If they don't reply, then call and mention to the receptionist that you emailed the journalist, and you'd like to know when the best time is to contact. You will be amazed at the information you will get. Receptionists are so used to people ringing them and asking for details and being in a panic. Can I just say here that receptionists in media outlets are amazing! They deal with everything and are your best sounding board if you can't get through to a journalist. You can ask the receptionist to leave a message for the journalist. **Also, the receptionist may be able to tell you whether or not your tactics are doing you more harm than good.** They are there to field all the calls and manage information flow, so they know a lot more than you think!

This chapter's main aim is to get you seeing things differently, thinking about what it's like to work as a journalist. If there is a small team in a newsroom then knowing that means you need to send in your story with more time built-in in advance of when you need to get it featured. A smaller team means fewer resources and means these journalists have a lot more jobs to get done in their average day.

Sometimes there is no good reason

There are times when a publication will make you want to give up. You follow all the instructions, you have a good release, a good photo captioned correctly, you send it in at a good time with lots of notice and your story still doesn't get published. Remember, your story will not be the only one that didn't make it. And remember with the changes happening so rapidly in traditional media as a result of online media, it is possible that the newsroom team may be just trying to keep their main beats covered and if they have time, they will do your story or source it out to a freelancer.

In a newspaper/magazine, whether mainly traditional, online or both, there can be a lot of by-lines, and you may be asking yourself why one of these people can't do your story. You wouldn't be the first that thinks there must be a lot of reporters in there. However, not all of them work there. Many are freelancers who write one article a week. Only a small portion of them are staff journalists. Same goes for national publications. They tend to outsource to freelancers they have a relationship with at times when they need help.

Or, you may just have gotten unlucky. There was just no space. Try Again. Send the release again but change it this time. Mention something different in your email about it or highlight an interesting fact about your pitch. Don't just resend it or forward it back on again. Show that you've realised it wasn't included last week but this week you are pitching it again with a fresh outlook and with a new angle. You can also ask the journalist/advertising executive or receptionist if there is an upcoming time that is better for your content to get featured and if you are happy to wait and can wait, then I suggest you do. It shows that you have given yourself plenty of time and are not last minute about these things. You will most likely get well considering you are in early.

The power of the follow-up and the follow-on

When your release doesn't make it, go buy that newspaper and do a breakdown of it. Look at the stories that made it and read them. Okay, so you didn't make it this time but is there a story in there that you have an angle on or a follow up to? It is common for people who are starting off to piggyback on other stories. Reactive PR is one of the best ways to get publicity and to build a story generation culture within your business. Recognising when you have a follow-up, or a follow-on story is a valuable skill. Always try to think if you have one and how best to tell it by linking it with previous coverage you've gotten or by making it relatable to a recently published story.

Once you get going, you may find that another business starting out doing publicity may need to piggyback on your story. If you can, elevate others and lift them up. You never know how valuable media publicity is to another business until you are benefitting from it yourself.

Editors in particular love follow-up stories. Readers do too. Readers always want to know what happened next. Editors want follow-ups, especially if their outlet broke an exclusive story. They don't want stories to be one-hit wonders. You could be that follow-up story that every journalist loves. Popular stories in particular are always good to have follow-ups to. If you can fit your story into a follow-up piece, you stand a good chance.

Give yourself three tries at getting featured for one story. Your follow-up emails should have something extra to add to the story. Therefore, you need to think at least 4 months in advance, and this is the very minimum. You will need to build relationships in this time also, so you need to mark out time for this. A relationship isn't built on the basis of one or two emails.

Following up on your story or following on from another can involve one or some of the following:

- Allow yourself time for anything a reporter might ask you to do or arrange. Like, can he/she interview the CEO (he/she may be on holidays or away for a portion of time)

- A reporter might want to take a different angle on the story. Are you happy with that? You may need time to think about it and to discuss it with management.

- A journalist may want to get some photos taken with their photographer. Who do you want in those photos and are they all around or contactable over the next few weeks?

- A journalist might say that he or she is interested in the story and wants to do an interview but won't be able to do it for two weeks as their schedule is jam-packed. Are you available then?

If you are sending in a piece for consideration, you need to be available during that period. Don't tell a journalist that you are not ready to go just yet and can they call back. You need to be ready to do interviews from the moment you press send on your press release.

A journalist may want you to go away and get more information which can take a lot of time. The piece you sent in may be similar to a piece they ran previously, and they will need to find a different angle. Any of the above can eat into your lead-in time to get your story into the newspaper/magazine/broadcast outlet. Think about a myriad of things that could happen and give yourself ample time to deal with them.

Pro tip

So many people are put off by media outlets because they can sometimes place you under a lot of pressure to get information and to get it quick. If you give yourself enough lead-in time, you will be able to deal with any requests without adding enormous pressure to your current workload. This is why I encourage you to pitch with 4-5 months of a lead-in time as you will have time to deal with things that crop up with ease and with a clear head. This is different for Reactive PR (piggybacking). This is more immediate as you are reacting to something already published.

Like I said before, giving yourself enough time is everything. Make it a priority. You will thank yourself that you did as oftentimes a journalist may be interested but might not get around to getting back to you. By allowing yourself time to contact again and politely asking if they are interested in your release, you are offering them another bite at the cherry and also giving yourself another shot at getting coverage, which could boost your business.

Come up with ideas that help the journalist

This is something that I wish people would do more of. If the journalist is given 2-3 angles that your content covers and it meets the content that they write, then you are winning on all fronts. Explain why you think your content will help readers and at the same time help the journalist. To do this well, come up with 2-3 ideas about where you think your content could fit. Don't just rely on the journalist to do all the work. You want to be featured. You need to do the work to get featured. Say why you think your story would fit great in a particular section. Even go as far as to say that these are reasons why you feel it could be a good fit.

After a major news story breaks, you could email the journalist that you know covered it and ask if they would be interested in any follow-ups you can offer. List them in bullet point format so they can scan the email quickly.

Journalists are human too

I worked as a senior court reporter and have covered gruesome stories and ones I still think about even now. I also covered inquests, and these can also be really tough to listen to and write about. I knew back then that the last thing I wanted to see after a full day in court is a press release about a business pitching me something, a call about the press release and another email asking why I haven't got back. I've had a tough day. My head is fried. I covered courts towards the end of the week mostly so if this press release was sent into me earlier, the chances are I would have been more amenable to reading it and therefore deciding on whether to contact or follow up. By sending it in on a day when I'm at a court all day, you are most likely not going to grab my attention, at least not straightaway.

Remember, journalists are human too. They are just as likely to be affected by a gruesome court story or inquest as you would be, but they have to put their feelings aside and write the story in a balanced way. A feat that isn't always easy and even seasoned journalists can find this hard at times. Journalists hear the most crazy, shocking things.

I've covered horrific court cases and it takes a bit of time afterward to get your head around it all and write the story. Also, keep in mind that a serious court case could be happening over a week or many weeks or months. The information can be difficult to digest. The journalist covering it may also be doing reports for other media outlets including radio and television. They will be repeating information again and again, reliving the case details numerous times. No matter how often a journalist goes to these kinds of court cases, they never get any easier. A journalist finds their way to cope and to get their job done in a balanced and impartial way because this is a hugely important part of the job.

So, when you think of all this, your press release will have to wait until after courts, inquests, and any other major stories are written up. It is just the way it goes. That is unless you are the major story of the day. Then, things are different. This is where you need to know the areas your journalist covers so you can gain a little understanding about what they might be doing in their week.

Media outlets and shows are made up of news stories that happen to the people that live around you. People read about people. They don't read about products without seeing them relate to how people have used and benefitted from them. They want to read about things that happen to people and how lucky they are that these things are not happening to them or they wish they were happening to them. Journalists are the same. They want to read about what is happening to the people around them.

Oh, and one last thing

Get to know the name of the journalist you are sending to. Get the spelling of their name right. Can you remember my last name and how it is spelt? I'd be rich if I got money for every time someone got it wrong. Coffee, Cossey, Cofey, Coofey, Coffeey. I could go on. (Its Coffey by the way!) When a journalist has come back from a heavy day at the courts, then they open your email and you have spelled their name wrong or addressed it to a competitor, you have let's say started off on the wrong foot!

Don't CC a ton of different journalists in one email and address it to the first journalist you have on the list (Despite new privacy rules, this still happens). Just don't. Take the time to send them individually and make it personal to each one. You will be tempted to send the same email to all of them but don't. Journalists see through this. Tailor it. Change it up a little to include something about the publication you are pitching, a story that the journalist just wrote. Yes, it is time consuming but that is why you need to be realistic and target 3-5 publications to start with.

I never forget those that tailor their email to me and make it personal. And yes, it can still get deleted if it isn't relevant. It can be disheartening to not hear back after putting in so much effort but try again. I once got an email that was addressed to a competitor but at the end stated, 'if any of the other journalists would like to cover this, please contact me.' Please, please don't do this. It's a sure-fire way to get remembered for all the wrong reasons.

And finally! Don't be overly eager. Your story may just not be that interesting to a wider readership. Don't pester journalists about your story. This isn't a good look for anyone, especially someone who is trying to grow a business.

CHAPTER 12

TYPES OF PRESS RELEASE

The press release is still the main way that journalists like to receive content. Although other methods of contacting journalists are growing in popularity, close to 40% of 3,000 journalists surveyed by Cision Media said that a press release remains their preferred way of getting your story idea.

The pitch email is one that I also like, in particular for major television, radio and some national print outlets. Once you build relationships, you will start to see what each journalist prefers. Don't limit yourself to the press release or pitch email. Remember the list I spoke about in Chapter 3 The Routes You Can Take, where I outlined numerous other ways to get your story out there. There are times too when a story merits a different approach. As a way of testing what gets reaction, utilising other methods is a good way to do this. Trying any of these other methods can also be a way of energising your team and reigniting their efforts in searching for media publicity ideas especially if previous efforts have not reaped rewards. Let's get back to the release!

This chapter focuses on the 8 types of press releases. In the following chapter, Chapter 12, I will go through the structure of a press release. Right now, I want to tell you about the 8 different types and why it is important to know which one most suits the type of story you want to tell.

8 types of press release

Okay, so you might have thought that one size fits all when it comes to press release writing. And this is the case mostly as the structure tends to follow a certain pattern for all. However, it is good to know how to frame your release, so it fits into one of the 8 types that I have identified below.

General News Release:

This is the most commonly used one. The idea behind it is to get featured online and offline using a format that has been around for a long time. General news releases can include things like winning an award or contest. Or stories like winning a new contract or joining up with another business on a new venture. This type of release leads with your hook and then you need to give details about the who, what, where, and when.

Launch Press Release:

You have a launch of a product or service or you are launching a new idea in your area of expertise. This type of press release is designed to clearly give details of the when, what, where, why, and how of your launch. The launch is your hook. The goal of this press release is to have the specifics so clear that the journalist will grasp them at a quick glance at the news story. It doesn't have to be a physical launch. You can also send a release for an online launch. Invite the journalist too!

The details of the event should be front and centre, not buried in the release somewhere, making it hard to find. It also helps to have them all in one place in the release so the journalist can place them as a highlighted section within the story. Punchy and short sentences work best. Use a list or bullet point format that gets details of the launch across clearly and succinctly.

Product Press Release:

You have a new product that you are announcing to the world. Congrats! This has some overlap with the launch press release if you are having a launch party for it. But, if you are announcing its upcoming availability to the world and factoring in a pre-order lead-in (which I recommend you have a pre-launch period of at least 2-3 months), then this press release works very well. The main difference between this and the launch release is that the product's details are front and centre (now you can have these in the launch release as well but make sure it doesn't become too busy and cluttered). If you are doing any fundraising for a charity on the back of your sales, then mention this early in the release too.

The main focus is on the product's release, when and where people can get it. What it does, how it is different from other products you have (if you have any) or others on the market. If this is your first product, state that. People are always encouraged by others and are interested in businesses releasing their first product. Journalists are also keen to be the first one to "discover" you. Try to get some quotes from someone who has tried it out ahead of its release. This also places more focus on the new things your product achieves. The new journey you are taking people on is an angle. You can do a Product Press Release followed by a Launch Press Release.

Event Press Release:

You are bringing a top celebrity to town. Or you are organising the first event that highlights an issue in your area of expertise. Or you have got together experts to discuss a hot topic. Great! The goal of an Event Press Release is to have the exact details of what is happening at the event clearly reprinted by the media outlets you send it to. A journalist will want to have the details so clearly outlined to them that they can copy and paste it into the story or onto an online post. Have good photos of your guests, CEO, or celebrity. Have some quotes from them so people know what to expect from the event.

Some details to include:

- Celebrity name and photo
- Open to public or not
- Cost of tickets
- Doors open at what time
- Where people can get tickets
- Seated or standing
- Disabled access
- Journalist's area or not (this is only for the journalist's information)

Think bullet points again for simplicity. If you are finding that your press release is looking too text heavy, then bolding different points of focus can work well.

New Hire/Celebrated Employee/CEO Press Release:

This type of release deals mainly with changes within your workforce like a new CEO taking over, an employee has been promoted or you have taken on a new employee and want to announce it to the media and your audience. This is typically reserved for high-level positions in management but if you have a release that details someone who has been working for your business for 20 years, what I call a "celebrated employee", then this is just as valid a story as a new CEO.

This press release type includes an extensive biography (you should clear this with the person being featured), some quotes from them about their new job/role, and what they hope to bring to the role and how they are looking forward to furthering the business and dealing with clients. At least one photo should be included. It should be professionally taken and not one from a social media outlet as those images are compressed and not of a high enough resolution. You can also include a more candid type of shot, depending on the type of business you run or how you are telling the story. If you have a business that has employees dressing in smart but casual clothes, you should try to make sure this is reflected across the images of the workforce from the top down.

The Expert Press Release:

You have someone in your business, or you are that person that is an expert in your field, and you want to announce this to the media. This person is a go-to source on this subject matter and details of their expertise are the focus of this release. This can include work they have done, education, research, interviews they have done, books they've written, articles written. Build up a picture of their expertise as this is what this release is for.

Some quotes from others who can vouch for their expertise is also important. A photo will be included. Also, state that they are available for interviews. Include the contact details of the expert.

Endorsement Press Release:

You have just received an endorsement from a celebrity, or you have just signed a celebrity or well-known person onto your team. This is similar to the Expert Press Release in that you will include some biographical details, but this release focuses on the celebrity and why their endorsement of you is worthy of a new story.

The celebrity should be forefront in the press release along with a photo. Include quotes from the celebrity and if possible have them available for interviews. This press release highlights your partnership and your future endeavours together.

Charity Press Release:

You have partnered with a charity and now is the time to give your work together some visibility. While you may have announced your partnership in a launch type press release, this type of release is different in that it involves the intricacies of why you came together and what you do together. In this, you will need photos of activities done and money raised, if any. And you will also need quotes from both your business and the charity. This will involve a campaign where the two organisations come together, and both do publicity to promote the partnership.

This isn't about selling anything. This press release promotes the good work you do to help those in need. You can put product details in there if you are giving them away to the charity for free. But be cautious about being overly salesy in this type of release. This is meant to have a feel-good community factor. You are showing your non-business side here and how you help others in a charitable way. It is about showing a different side to your business. Oftentimes, businesses will promote their charity work heavily to gain traction in the media so they can bring the focus into the business at a later date.

There will be times when you will only use 1-2 types of release. No matter what which one you use, make sure that the most pertinent information relating to the type of release is at the top and all the rest follows it. The next chapter deals with what you need to put into a release and how to write it.

CHAPTER 13

THE PRESS RELEASE

STRUCTURE AND WHAT TO INCLUDE

A press release or news release remains the standard way to introduce yourself to the media. When starting off, I always recommend having a good press release and having it so well laid out and the content so clear that there is no confusion.

A good press release: What makes it good?

Firstly, a press release offers you the best way to introduce yourself to the media. You can try all the other ways as you start to build traction and find other ones that work for you. But to start with, this is best. The press release is how many make their first connection with a journalist or media organisation. It has never been more vital to get this right as journalists work under huge pressure while some are facing uncertainty around the way traditional media operates and changes are constantly happening around this issue. Despite the importance of social media, to get your story into the right hands, you need a good press release.

Writing a press release is different to how you write for social media. A press release needs to tell your story in a certain way, has a structure that you must follow, is well crafted, follows some basic guidelines, has a story, and has contact details. There is overlap here, of course, but once you start to write releases, you will begin to see the differences. The story part is the one part that people find the most difficult. There are times when what people think is a story is inevitably not a story in the journalist's eyes. Oftentimes, a journalist will pick out a piece in the press release and focus on that and the story may well be about something that is not what you had intended. With that in mind…

Be happy with everything you've included

My first tip is to be happy with everything you've put into the release. Ask yourself if you would be happy if the journalist took a different angle to the one you sent in? Would you be happy if they took some detail further down the release and used that in the headline and across social media? **Everything in the release should be something you would be happy seeing in a headline.** If you follow that principle, you won't be upset at seeing your press release get totally changed and swapped around. I have seen people become shocked when they look through a media publication and can't find their story. I point to them that it is there; it just isn't the story they sent in. The journalist saw a different angle and went with that instead. Be happy with everything knowing that it will get changed.

Contacting via social media

To receive a well-written press release is a rare thing nowadays. People send a quick email via Facebook or Twitter or in some cases use the Subject Line of an email only to send in details (yes, this happens). While contacting via social media is okay in certain circumstances, for a first-time pitch, you should email to the journalist's work email. Some journalists have their email online and have their DMs open, making it easy to contact them. They are open to pitches via social media. Others, however, are not. Don't be tempted to send a message if they aren't open to it.

Here's why: A Facebook or Twitter message can first appear like you are trying to be too familiar with the person. Or you are doing things at the last minute and are desperately emailing to get their attention. Instead, you should use social media as a way of getting to know the journalist you are sending to. After you have commented on some of their posts and shown an interest you can then message via social media if they request it. And you avoid looking too eager or coming across as a stalker! If you know that a journalist you are contacting is always on a certain social media channel, then you can be confident that they will see your message quickly. Mention in your email that you felt it merited contacting them on their social DMs. Don't make this a habit. This is fine for something urgent.

Of course, contacting via social media is fine if you have built up a relationship with this journalist and are actively following each other online. In the first instance, it is best to stick to the tried and trusted method – sending a well-written press release to the right person at their email address.

Logical story construction

In normal circumstances, the least you can do is sit down and put together your story in a logical way for a journalist to read.

Oftentimes, I found that those who don't do that are the people that come back and complain to the journalist that their story wasn't "done right" or "it wasn't what we thought you would do". But in the first instance, all you sent was a one-line message in a Facebook message, you posted it up on FB or Twitter and tagged a load of journalists. All these approaches are just not good enough. They don't give you a proper chance to get coverage and they leave the journalist with so many questions that it is easier for them to move on to the next story. And there is always the next story waiting to be told, and the next story could well be a better one. Pertinent details come first then look at your quotes, some background information and continue to develop your story from there.

White space

When you are putting your information together in a press release, try to let your paragraphs breathe. Put plenty of white space in there, use bullet points to break things up. Make it readable. Follow my earlier advice on press release types. I advise you to craft a professional email with all your details organised clearly. Construct it in a way that makes it easy to follow on a quick read and have your press release support your email. Don't assume that the journalist will open the press release. They will be looking for something that pertains to them in your email. Remember to give this plenty of space so a journalist can scan it quickly. Don't leave the journalist with more questions than answers. As a journalist, I spent a lot of time following up on a release because as I've said it is rare to receive one that has all the details needed for a story. Often, I've had to contact the person about the photos, the email will be unclear, the press release has many errors. I've gotten press releases that were unfinished drafts.

Often, a press release leaves more questions unanswered than answered. It has spelling errors or basic errors of clarity. It is sent to the wrong person. If you are lucky, the journalist you've sent it to will forward it on to the appropriate colleague. Or often he/she will shout across the room 'Jane, have you any interest in {whatever it is}'. And her reply can often be that she is too busy or that it doesn't sound interesting. This means that a decision about your story can be made in a nanosecond.

Think about the press release for a second – it is a blank canvas for you to stand out. It acts as one of the best and trusted ways for you to tell your story so make the most of it. I'm here to give you the confidence to go for it.

Elements of a press release

Forget getting every detail in there. Overloading your press release with unnecessary details is a sure way to confuse a journalist. A confused journalist will not take action. Get your angle first. Your press release shouldn't be many pages long. Two pages is plenty. I like to keep them to 500 words. At a push 700 is okay but anything over that is way too long. A bio can be included separately to this but keep it to 200 words. Keep these details in mind before you begin.

The Headline (also use this in the subject line of the email)

This goes across the top of your press release. And I recommend you use this in the subject line of your email with your area of expertise highlighted.

Example:
Work From Home: Top tips to keep your sanity and your health

intact

Make this sentence interesting and intriguing; have it start your narrative. Ask yourself this: What is the main angle of my story? What is the best angle I can offer about my launch, my business opening, my new hires, a celebrity endorsement, or a new collaboration? Make this the focus of your headline.

However, remember that the journalist may think otherwise. He/she often does and even after it is changed by a journalist it can get changed again at least 4 times. Think of your headline and email subject line as your invitation to read more. You are showing them that you've thought of an angle that is of interest to what they do, and this is something that they can work with.

Example:
Medical factory announces new jobs - *okay*
Medina Medical announces 100 new jobs - *better*

Example:
Medical factory closes after 40 years - *okay*
Medina Medical factory closes after 40 years as owners outsource to Asia - *better*

Sub-Headline

This should relate to your headline in some way. It needs to continue the narrative you have set up and begun. This is the line that goes underneath your Headline. It is normally in a smaller font size. It is not essential to include but I always encourage it if there is something you can say that bolsters your headline and gives the journalist another insight into why the story is worth doing. It acts as a way of adding to or explaining your main headline.

Both the headline and subhead should be punchy and catchy. But refrain from using lots of different font styles. This is very distracting. Avoid lots of colour too. Most text is printed in black and white and stick to that.

Example:
The factory needs new workers with expertise - *okay*
Company seeks people with research, engineering, and technical skills - *better*

The two together:

Headline: Medina Medical announces 100 new jobs
Sub-headline: Company seeks new employees with research, engineering, and technical skills

The above headline and sub-headline are related. It is easy for a journalist to see that this is a business story that needs to get in somewhere. They may follow up with a request for an interview. Now let's take another example using some information from earlier. I want to show you the difference between what you could have sent in and what a journalist will look for.

Example: **The press release format**

Headline: Medina Medical factory closes after 40 years as owners seek to diversify
Sub-headline: 800 employees given redundancy package this morning

A journalist, especially if they have done stories about this company before and they most likely will have seeing as it was around for 40 years, will be looking for more detail. And they may find it in the press release or request an interview. Most likely, the latter. This is a major story, and it will likely get more coverage than just one article.

Example: **What the journalist may write**

Headline: Medina Medical to close after 40 years as owners outsource to Asia
Sub-headline: 800 employees told the news via email

This is an example of where the two work really strong together from a story point of view. It is different to what was sent in, but I want to show you now that things get changed. Also, the fact that they were told via email is strong enough to use in a headline too depending on the tone of the article. In cases like this when a business closes, it is important to monitor coverage and be ready to respond to any stories or correct any serious inaccuracies.

Introduction:

This is where you need to nail down your story. This is your way in to further explaining your reason for sending in this release. While the headline and subject line act as an invite to get the journalist to come into your world, your introduction is the handshake that makes them say yes to doing your story. It can follow on from your headline and sub-headline to further explain them. Or you could start with a striking quote, a fact from research you've done in-house or discovered or a newsworthy angle on a current story.

Example:

People with certain skills are being encouraged to apply for one of the new 100 jobs that have just been announced at Medina Medical – *okay*

One hundred new jobs have been announced by Medina Medical at a time when unemployment levels in the city have doubled. The good news comes as.... – *better*.

You are announcing jobs but also linking it in with the problem of unemployment being high in the city. You will need to get some stats on unemployment figures which are easily received by your local Department of Jobs. They are also posted online, or you can find them in any of the local newspapers. Jobs being created or lost are always stories of interest to journalists.

You can think of your first paragraph as a summary of what is to come. If a person reads only this line, it should tell them enough information about the story.

Example:

Jobs are being announced today by Medina Medical as they launch a new product. – *okay*.

One hundred jobs are being created by Medina Medical who are unveiling a new product for heart disease sufferers. With the growing rate of heart disease (put in figures to back this up)... - *better*

Can you see how one element of the press release always follows on from the one before? When writing the opening paragraph, try to think of how it would read or sound in a media outlet. Think short sentences or a quote that could be worth using. Something catchy is the key here. You can lead with a good quote from someone on your team or an ideal customer who has tried your product and found benefits. Leading with a quote has to be worth it. The quote has got to stand out.

Example:

"It has added 10 years to my life," says a dad-of-three who was one of the first to try a new product made by Medina Medical.

Here, you would go on to give his name, where he lives (not exact address) and some more details about him, his family and how it has changed his life. You would also get more quotes from his partner and/or one of his children. You will also need a photo. One of him on his own and a family one. It goes without saying that making sure his family are comfortable with this is important from the outset. If he is the only focus, then you've still got a good story. As you go down the press release, you want to prioritise your information flow. The information should flow from the most important detail to the least.

The body of the release

Try to keep this a well-balanced mix of informative content and quotes. When you use a quote, try to have that quote related to the text that has gone before or that is coming after. It isn't essential but it helps with flow and readability. A press release with poor quotes is a pretty boring one and will be tough to bring to life on the page. This is an example of how the two can link together.

Example:

The product is designed to widen the arteries of the heart and thereby relieve pressure put on this vital organ. "Patients will benefit hugely from the product because it will keep their hearts healthy and strong. It will prolong their lives." – *good. It is putting patients at the centre of the story and it isn't going into the finer details too early. Those can come later in the release.*

Quotes:

Here are some notes about quotes that I'd like you to keep in mind.

Quotes should differentiate facts from opinion.

Quotes should serve a purpose and not be overused.

Try to use your strongest ones at the top and slowly introduce others further on. Like I said in a previous chapter, look at what you've got and find the best 1-2 sentences and lead with them. Be selective and hold ones that are not relevant for another release.

Keep them short. 15-20 words per quote is enough. Keep them punchy and eye catching. Think of the journalist with little time scanning through for a good quote that they can use. You want them to be able to find it.

They should show personality, commitment, drive. They should speak directly to the reader. You should also have all the details of the person quoted. Are they the CEO, the Marketing Director, the Sales Director, etc. Good quotes will get used. Keep this in mind at all times. Put the name of the person quoted and their title after the quote. The quote that is the most interesting should come first.

Example:

"It was time for this company to diversify to suit our changing audience and to try new things. We wanted for a long time to change things around and we are constantly researching new things and methods. Our team had worked on this new device for a long time and today we can finally say that we made it and we are creating new jobs to make it happen," Nicholson said. – *long-winded, doesn't say anything much. Boring and a definite turn-off for a journalist.*

"Today is the culmination of five years of research that has been completed by our team. This product will help save the lives of many people with this heart condition and it also creates jobs for people who are skilled in this area," CEO Ben Nicholson said. It describes more about the product, it has the full name of CEO, it is short and to the point – *better. Readers want to know how this product changes lives. They are not all that interested in how great the company is.*

"We made it! Five years of research and we now have a solution to the heart problems of over 1 million people," said CEO of Medina Medical Ben Nicholson. – *better. Readers get a sense of achievement and of the amazing work this product is going to go on to do.*

It is easy to use a lot of quotes in a release but be picky. This can be difficult in certain industries and certainly within the health industry where extra caution is taken regarding quotes. But try to keep your eye on what you need to state so you always stay true to what the product while also making it relatable to the journalist and his/her audience. The CEO might want to talk about a lot of things that have happened but always remember:

One idea = one press release

Many ideas = scattered approach = confusion = delete

Keep it focused on one essential idea. You can always use the other quotes in another release or a follow-up piece. Think of other stories that you can build around these quotes. When picking someone to quote, it isn't always necessary to have the CEO, though he or she may want to be quoted. Also, be mindful that you will need to edit their quotes to make them readable. It is good to explain this at the start so the CEO/spokesperson (if you are dealing with one) is aware that you may need to change them. However, you will also be showing them the final edits.

Your spokesperson is the person the press will want to interview on seeing the story if they deem it newsworthy. Many radio journalists seek out stories for their news slots and programmes in both national and regional newspapers. So, you must have someone that is a confident speaker and speaks well on behalf of the company. You need someone who can deal well with their nerves and would be happy to go on camera if asked. It is a good idea to mention this to the person who is being quoted so they know that this can happen.

How do you know what to put at the top?

- What is the newest information?
- Have you won anything noteworthy?
- Are you launching something?
- Did you recently launch something, and it sold well? Any figures to back this up?
- Are you making high-value comments on a topical subject?
- Are you an expert in something and there is an issue in this area that people need to hear about? And are you in a position to speak about it?
- Did you struggle at something in your business, and you found a way to combat it that you would like to share? These types of stories are huge as they show readers how to get from A to B, how to go from a difficult situation to a positive one. And who doesn't want to read about how someone overcame a difficulty, a difficulty that they could potentially face too.

What I encourage people to do is to think about what has happened recently in the business or think about what is coming up in the business. This is where you could start if you are struggling to find a beginning. Prioritise that information and rate all the following information by how close it sits to the beginning, i.e., the part that you are using in your headline, sub-headline, and first paragraph. It doesn't have to be mind-blowing to get into the first paragraph. It doesn't have to be earth-shattering! It can be something like raising 100 dollars for charity by doing a simple thing in the office. How you make it relevant to readers is what matters.

Why is this important? If your press release is used, it is oftentimes the information that is close to the top that is read most. Your whole pitch is decided by what is in those first lines. Not the information that is close to the end.

PRO TIP: Don't hold off on sending your press release by trying to perfect your quotes. If the journalist feels they need to interview the person quoted, they will contact you to arrange. So, save yourself time and use quotes that are relevant to boost your press release.

How to build out your press release

Many struggle with this and are unsure what to include to build out your story. This is where having solid informative content comes into play. What do I mean by this? Important details about the company throughout the release can help do this.

Such as:

- When the company was formed
- Why it was formed
- What exactly it does
- Its start-up story
- About the company founders
- Testimonials
- How it has grown
- If it has won any awards or is in line for any
- Any expansion plans

Consider the details that add weight to your release. A word of caution here. Don't go on and on. A brief mention is what's needed and pick wisely. Think 2-3 sentences about ones on this list that relate. Ones that are essential to include are anything that puts you in the expert seat like things about the company's formation, awards won or shortlisted for, or a testimonial from someone well known in your area.

Going into further detail on these forms part of other stories, other press releases, other ways of keeping the conversation about your business going. You can include a bio at the end if you need to.
Anything that informs the journalist and hence the reader more about your business is what makes up the informative elements of your release.

A useful thing to have on your website is a Resources Section that you can share with journalists. You can have it password protected. Inside this section, you can have things like photos, testimonials, bios, background, anything that can help a journalist. Also have background information on a product but keep it short and relevant. Any videos that can tell the story about the company in 1-2 minutes are a great resource. Also, do the same for product videos. If you have an offer, put that in here too. A journalist may want to include that offer in their story or as a reader giveaway.

Try to end strong

If you have event details (if it is a launch) put them both at the beginning and the end of your release. Oftentimes, in launch type stories, a journalist may like to use the dates and times of an event at the start and again as a recap at the end. So, make sure you give plenty of visibility to that.

- At the end of the press release, you will need to put **ENDS** in capital letters. This signifies the end of your release. All information above ENDS can be used. All information below ENDS cannot be used without being asked about first (This is something all journalists learn in college or from being on the job).
- After ENDS you will put all your contact details. These include yours and the person who is quoted. If for instance, the person quoted is needed for a quick radio interview and you happen to be on holiday or away from your desk, having their number there means you don't miss that opportunity. But obviously, you need to make sure that person is okay with that.
- Always read over it, put it away for a few hours or a day if possible, and read over it again. You'll be surprised at what details are missing or what words are spelt incorrectly.

Knowing the journalist and your audience is the key to this. If you send in a release that is overly hard to understand, and keep in mind that journalists get these all the time, then needless to say it will take longer for your release to get read and to feature. It will take too much time to understand. It may cause it to be deleted because it is not clear. If it is not clear to the journalist receiving it, then they will automatically believe that it will not be clear to a regular reader who will not have as much time as they do to digest the information.

You will need to get clearance from management for the release, if required, so factor in time for this. Allow for changes but if you feel that the release is going down a very formal route or if it is becoming very tech or business heavy, then it is up to you to put your foot down if you feel this will not work with the journalist you are sending it to. The opposite also works in this case. If the release is lacking vital tech or business information, then it is not going to resonate with the journalist targeted to receive it.

Some last tips:

Don't place too much emphasis on your headline. So many people delay sending in their release because they feel that the headline is not good enough. The headline will get changed. It could get changed three times or more. Once by the journalist, another time by the sub-editor and finally by the editor. The headline you put on your press release/photocall notice or pitch will ultimately be the thing that grabs a journalist's eye or an editor's eye. Let that be enough. You will need to think carefully about what headline you are going to put on your piece and if it reflects the content that runs underneath it. Once it reflects your content, go with it, and send it. Don't wait. The longer you wait, the longer you will doubt yourself.

Don't go for a shocking headline or one that doesn't reflect your business or content. It must be authentic and tell your story. It doesn't have to be jaw-dropping or shocking to have an impact. I would say that thanks to the gluttony of shocking headlines, people are getting tired and sick of them. I believe journalists know by a headline how genuine your copy is and will be interested to read on. You want to get them to read it but not throw their eyes to heaven knowing you went for a shocking headline, but your copy doesn't follow through on it. Finally, **use the active voice, instead of the passive.** This helps bring to life your story on the page and helps to place the journalist into the heart of your story.

CHAPTER 14

THE PITCH EMAIL

Previously, I stated that there are 8 types of press release and that the press release remains the go-to method to get publicity. However, there are times when a pitch email is the better way to go. I advise using this method when your story/follow-on/opinion/comment has a quick timeframe before it is due to expire. I also advise using a pitch email when people send their story to a national television reporter or a radio journalist. And also, sometimes to major national and international newspapers and magazines. Once you start to contact journalists in your area of expertise, you will begin to discover what method they prefer to receive information.

Some Pointers First

A pitch email is a shorter version of a press release - 200 words maximum (more details on this later). When you are pitching and trying to stick out among the hundreds of emails a journalist gets every day, you are better off:

- Being concise and to the point

- Having your pitch email tailored to what the journalist writes about and giving them everything they need in the body of an email. There is nothing else to read. That's it.

Prepare and quit the hype

If there is one thing journalists hate, it is hype for hypes' sake. The eagerness to put in lots of hype language is something I've often seen in my time as a journalist. I've seen it regularly in all forms of content but more so in the pitch email format because people feel they need to do this in order to get attention. Hype is a turn-off, especially if it is over-hyped. Good stories don't need hype. They write themselves usually. Words like "the best ever", "the highest ever", "You'll never believe". All of this type of hyped language is off-putting. Be straight and to the point. Journalists get these kinds of emails all the time. Having hyped statements makes the work harder for them. They will need to ask: Well, is this the best ever? Is this the hottest new moisturizer? They will have read this a million times and have been disappointed as many more times. Let the journalist decide whether or not they want to state it was the "best moisturiser they've ever used. They will have read this a million times and have been disappointed as many more times. Let the journalist decide whether or not they want to state it was the "best moisturiser they've ever used for acne prone skin". Having the journalist say it instead of you makes it a stronger statement.

Don't put a load of links into your copy and state that this is an unbelievable video, or "you need to click on this now". This is enough for the journalist to click delete and possibly block you. Journalists get this type of clickbait content all the time and for many it is an instant delete. What you need to spend your time on is getting their name correctly spelt and doing your research. This is vital. Some research can be easily put together by reading some of their previous articles and finding out what types of stories the journalist likes to cover and post about on social media.

Listen for a while

At the beginning and throughout your media publicity journey, it is a good idea to listen for a period of time. Listen to what is going on in your field, any reactions you should be aware of, any inspiration you can glean just by absorbing content and listening. This is a great exercise that I encourage you to do when you can.

Twitter is a great place to get details of stories, trends, and the names and emails of journalists (some share their emails on Twitter). And it is also a good place to just listen for a while. Listen to what makes the journalists you want to target tick. Building relationships on here is a good place to start. Have some conversations on here without pitching. Start to gather information about where things are at in your field, what the hot topics are. This is particularly important if you are starting your media publicity or have not been doing publicity for a short while.

You only need a few – 3-4 to start with

I see this all the time. You draft a pitch email and blast it out to 50 journalists. It is easy; you just forward it on again and again. Sometimes you forget to take the "FW" off the email! Even if you don't do this, journalists know it is an email that is being widely sent around. They know this by reading it. Remember they get hundreds of emails every day, they are email savvy. So, start with 3-4 journalists that you feel are within your reach and would be interested in what you have got to say and draft a different email to each of them. And I mean totally different. It may be the same product/launch/service you are trying to promote but draft a different email for each. I'll go into more detail on this later in this chapter.

Having meaningful relationships with 3 journalists is a lot better than mediocre relationships with many. A journalist gravitates towards those who put the time and effort into their pitch email, and they will recognise this instantly. Write your email knowing that its recipient is time poor. Journalists are time poor and under huge pressure to get, research and write stories that have something to say to their readers. They don't have time to read a bunch of text. Write it in a way that it is easy to skim through with some bold throughout to highlight anything of major significance that you want them to see. A journalist reading through hundreds of emails who then goes to open your one, will want to know straightaway if this is a story for them and then they will lead the conversation about where it will go. Make the email super easy to read.

The pitch email is a time-saving exercise for you and for the journalist

Sending a pitch email saves you a heck of a lot more time than writing a press release, because once interested the journalist will get back to ask about the angle they want to take, and you can go from there instead of writing a 500-word release that they might not even open. Nowadays and especially in major media outlets and in radio and television, journalists want to see a relatable pitch that is aimed directly at what they cover. **A pitch is a shorter version of a press release, but they are totally different things.** By all means use the information in the press release but tailor it and keep it short.

Don't shorten your press release and send a summary of that instead. Do this:

- Tailor your pitch email directly to that journalist's area of expertise.
- A pitch is straight to the point, no need for filler, in fact, don't put any filler in there.
- It is a short piece of text, sent in the body of an email with white space used well to make it easy to read quickly. Links are included in this too.
- Word count should be no longer than 200 words. That's it, any longer and the journalist will be put off.

Keep the journalist's eyes on your email by keeping it short. That way, they can decide whether or not your story is right for them in the two minutes it takes for them to read it. By getting them to read to the end, you are already far ahead of everyone else sending in pitches that don't have a point, no news angle and are way too long.

The 4 elements to a pitch email

Journalists get hundreds of pitches every single day. Can you imagine what that is even like to see every day? It is pretty overwhelming, and a busy journalist will first want to weed through and start hitting the delete button. Let me ask you something: So, when you open your email, the first thing you want to do is clear it right? Same for journalists. They want to clear their inbox and only keep what they need. And you need to stay on the list of what they need.

Put yourself in their shoes. How wonderful is it to open an email and in 4 paragraphs the journalist has all it needs to decide on your story! Already, you have perked them up by not having loads of text, links, photos, videos, pdf reports and the list goes on.... When you pitch a story, it is hard to not put loads of text in there because you want to give the journalist enough reasons to cover your story. But, by putting in too much detail and not having a focus, you are doing yourself a disservice and not offering a distinct angle. You are losing out by not having a single focus to your reason for contacting a journalist.

The 4 Elements

Element 1 - Greet the journalist - by name

Greet the journalist by name and state anything you liked about a previous story or you have a follow-up or an expert willing to talk about an issue that they have previously written about. Jump straight into your reason why. Your introductory point is your news hook. This is the most important thing about your story. Save yourself time by not doing any long intro or stating your credentials at this point. There is no need for big introductions about who you are, what you've done and achieved. Nope and Nope. Remember, this isn't about you upfront, it is about your story and how it helps readers and viewers.

And talking about the weather (unless it relates to your story) or how there is a cold spell coming in Germany has no relation to what you are doing and for me personally I never saw a need for this type of introduction. The most important thing here is the piece of information you've been dying to give away, the most valuable. This states why you are contacting them because you have a story that is newsworthy. All the other things like bio, credentials will come once you have a story that is worthy of getting put on the news list.

Element 2 – what do you want the journalist to do

Are you beginning to see that writing to a journalist is totally different to any other kind of writing? The next part of your email states what you want the journalist to do with this information. They will also have their own ideas, but you need to offer them one here. Think of this like your Call to Action (CTA). Ask yourself what would you most like the journalist to do and how are you going to help them do this? Don't offer them an 800-page report to read or a 2-hour video to watch. Give them a summary of it in a link, not the full report attached to the email. You want to keep them engaged; they are seeing at the bottom of their screen right now emails coming in and maybe one from someone they've been waiting to hear back from.

You want them to wait and read more of your email. You don't want them to roll their eyes on reading that you want them to read a long report. The CTA is what you want them to do. Make this as clear as possible. Don't go down the route of being vague here. You want them to interview your CEO, you have an event lined up for Valentine's Day, you have your special guest reveal or your company is about to sponsor a major competition. Hand-hold them. Walk them through and keep them interested.

Element 3 – the news element(s)

Why is your story newsworthy? This element is where you state clearly why your story is worthy of being featured. This can be the big stumbling block and I see many unfinished emails because it isn't clear enough why this is newsworthy. The best way to do this is by looking at your story through the eyes of those you have helped and those you can help. Relate your story to your audience to find its newsworthiness. Go back to the reason why you decided to choose this story for your pitch.

This paragraph lays out why your email has the basis of a story worthy of being featured. Look at this as a follow-on sentence to what has gone before. You are building out a picture of whys here. Let one element build on the previous one. Show the journalist the value of what you are offering, share a statistic, share what differentiates you or your story. Share a link to a survey or a post you've written. Share where you think your story fits into the news agenda and make it relevant to what is happening now or in the future. This is the sentence that makes them say YES.

Element 4 – a strong closing and a little extra if you have it

Sign off. Yes, you are finished. But hold on! This is a super important element. You've got them to read this far. Well done. But we are not finished just yet. You need to end strong. Here, you need to thank the journalist, mention your CTA again and include contact details so you can be easily contacted. Include links to your website and socials and also to any previous publicity you have got especially if it a major publication or if it is a story that got a lot of attention. Mention the views it got and likes and shares.

By mentioning your CTA again, you are doing something majorly important. Sometimes journalists just read the top and tail of an email and only then read the middle. Putting your call to action again gives you a much better chance that they will know what you want them to do. Always include a phone number. If a journalist is on a tight deadline, they may not be as inclined to do your story if they have to write an email and wait for you to get back. They will be more inclined to pick up the phone and speak to you to get a clearer sense of whether they can do the story in the timeframe they have.

A phone number is even more vital if you are sending to a tv journalist because they will want to call you to arrange an interview. TV is a now type of medium. It isn't a medium that will wait. So, if you are not ready to jump right after sending the email, then don't send it. Get ready first and then send. Can you see how writing pitch emails over time could actually be enjoyable but also really quick? (maybe not but that's okay).

There will be times when you will not need all of these elements. But this is how best to think about the optimal way to get a journalist's attention. Now, let's look at the structure in more detail.

Pitch email structure

Reminder: A pitch is a much shorter version of a press release. But they are totally different things. You must get across the essence of your story in 4-5 paragraphs in the BODY of the email and be ready to go on air or be interviewed the minute you press send. So many people forget that pitching to television is hugely different from other mediums. TV is now. It is right now. So, you need to be ready right at the moment you pitch. You have 200-250 words to play with. You also have the subject line of your email. That is all. Journalists love good pitches. Television journalists in particular love reading the essence of a story in a short email and then deciding there and then whether to do something on it. Your media pitch needs to be:

- Timely
- Newsworthy
- Brief
- Structured
- Relevant

An example of a good pitch email

Hi Philip,

I just read your story on postpartum depression in new fathers. The story of Andy was really heart breaking. I specialise in this area, and I hear stories from fathers all the time about how they find fatherhood difficult but seem to have nowhere to turn to.

I'm Scott, and my company, Finding Fatherhood (LINK), offers counselling, support, and a range of resources for fathers to help them be happy and function on a day-to-day basis as the best dad they can be.

Recently, I worked with our regional healthcare providers to survey a sample of 300 fathers who had become dads in the last 18 months. The results were truly shocking and show that care needs to go into this area. New fathers revealed that their needs are not being met. Over half of them reported that they felt depressed in their first year as a father.

Here is a link to the survey summary – INSERT LINK

New fathers are telling us that they need preparation classes on becoming a dad, how to deal with the transition, as well as how to cope with relationship difficulties and sleep deprivation.

Let me know if you find our survey useful and if you want to use it in any of your upcoming articles. Look forward to reading your next piece.

Thank you for your time today,

Scott.

Underneath, put in link to the homepage of the site, Twitter handle, Facebook group, and any other relevant details. Include a short biography (150 words max). Any photos should be in a link not attachments. Include a telephone number.

This pitch email is 227 words. It has the four elements in four paragraphs with other information around it to support it. It is concise, to the point, and is relevant to what this journalist covers. This is a good example of what you could aim for with your pitch. You don't always need a survey or study. You can have a link to a post you've written, a book you are publishing, a link to your expert (LinkedIn or other social media).

Always give details – time, date (day, month, and year) of your event and the person who is organising it and their contact details. Don't be tempted to link to lots of places. A pitch is meant to be short and punchy, and it is best to keep it that way. One to two links is sufficient in the body of the email. If writing pitches are your strong point, then you can try this as your main way of contacting journalists. But be aware that they may want more details, like a press release, biography and so on, afterward. This is the best response you can hope to get as the journalist is keen to work with you and your pitch email has done its job! It has got the attention of the journalist. And that is an achievement with hundreds coming in every day.

There are different types of pitch emails and I am going to deal with them next. But suffice to say they all stick to the same formula and try to be as succinct as possible yet driven by good content and a knowledge of what makes a good story.

Pitch Email Types

In this section, I am going to first show you the pitch email (in italics) with a short introduction, go through the different elements it has and then say why I think it works.

Pitch Email Type 1

For when you are time poor and want to get started easily. This is short and sweet and is exactly what journalists need right now in a pitch.

Hi Emily,

Our company MomsInDesign has done a survey asking our 10,000 members if their businesses have gone up or down in revenue since COVID-19. Turns out 31% of them have seen their sales rise!

See the survey summary here: LINK

Seems like moms are really rocking the design space.

Let me know what you think.

Thanks for your time and I'm happy to answer any questions you have.

Sandra

PS: I have 2 women ready to tell their stories if this is of interest to you. Rachel is a 25-year-old mom of 2 who recently started her Etsy business and is already making 4 figures a month and working 4 hours a day. Breda lost her job during the pandemic and while nervous about going on her own, she has just set up her interior design consulting business and got her first client. Put links HERE.

Element 1 - Lead off - This first paragraph has who you are, the number of people surveyed and what your news hook is.

Element 2 – What you want the journalist to do: You want the journalist to view the link. Have the first 1-2 pages of the survey in a summary format. Make it easy!

Element 3 - Newsworthiness: Moms are bucking the trend. This is of interest as it goes against other reports stating that moms in business have suffered during the pandemic.

Element 4 - Sign off and a little extra: You are available to answer questions. And you have two women ready to talk which is always a good thing to tell a journalist. They will always go for the human angle first. Only tell the journalist that you are ready to offer this if you are really ready. Don't tell them this if you have to go off and ask a bunch of mothers afterwards.

A word about using PS at the end of an email: I like to use this from time to time as it makes it feel more tailored and friendly. Don't worry about this looking unprofessional. To me, it often helps to bring in some of your personality.

Why this one works

It is short and to the point. If you have targeted your journalists correctly, you should get a great response to this one. You didn't have a lot of time to research, but you have the journalist's name and their area of expertise. So, you are good to go. Test this email type against the others in this section. I'm a big believer in using this and one of the others and seeing which ones get the best responses.

PRO TIP: Don't go sending to hundreds of journalists. Start small and do the work well. That way you get to build meaningful relationships with journalists in your field of interest.

With this pitch email, the journalist can run a simple story on the survey alone. Or a short piece on the survey and focus more on the mothers. One mother may have a really good story, and this could turn into a feature or a story that is done in another issue after the survey is covered.

The journalist will want to ask you more questions about each of the mothers to decide what they want to do. Also, there may be other angles to the survey. Which you can tell the journalist if they call or email you asking for other angles. But have this in the survey summary. They may feel that just having an increase in their sales isn't enough of a news story. They will want more. Them wanting more is a sign that they are interested. Have other angles ready.

A survey offers many options. A good link to more information is what you ultimately need here. This can be in a Google Doc or a pdf stored on your site. If you are doing a survey, you need to make sure your figures are collated properly and that the survey's stats stand up to scrutiny. Ideally, it is good to do it with a reputable organisation. But for budget reasons this may not always be possible. If it turns out that you did it yourself, you may need to show exactly how you did it and how you collated the details.

PRO TIP: Always have a summary of your survey, report, newsletter, or industry talk. A journalist is time poor. They will read the full report but only if it merits it.

Pitch Email Type 2

A more personalised approach: For when a personalised approach is needed to build relationships faster

Hi Emily,

I read your feature about Felicity Fairbank who just started her own business after losing her job and her house. Her story really resonates with our MomsInDesign company as we support women in design businesses, and many have faced difficulties.

We recently did a survey of our 10,000 members asking them various questions about their business struggles and what they need help with.

The survey summary is available here: LINK. Among the issues highlighted by members include having a support network of fellow women at various stages of their business to having affordable childcare to make it easier for women to follow their business dreams.

Let me know if you find our study interesting. You'll see at the beginning that we have highlighted the major elements of the study.

Two mothers (PUT LINKS TO THEM) are ready to be interviewed if this interests you. I felt this might be of more interest to the Spotlight Section that you write for.

Women need our support more than ever. I want to thank you for your work in this area.

Sandra

Element 1 - Lead off: This first paragraph highlights so many things that journalists like. You have done research; you've read a previous story and you are relevant.

Element 2 – What you want the journalist to do: You want the journalist to view the link. Have the first 1-2 pages of the survey in a summary format. Have this the first thing the journalist sees when they click the link.

Element 3 - Newsworthiness: This time, the angle is different. You are highlighting issues that moms are facing and naming two gives you a better chance of getting the journalist to want more.

Element 4 - Sign off and a little extra: This is important because no journalist has time to read a full 100-page study. Having a good ending that makes a point works best.

Why this one works

This example shows that you have done more research into the outlet you are pitching and type of content the particular journalist writes. This is an important thing to do, and it helps in the long run to have a list of targeted journalists that you have or are building relationships with. If your pitch isn't tailored, then I can guarantee you that it will be instantly deleted and not even opened.

This pitch is about having an angle on an already published story the journalist did. This is what we call newsjacking or piggybacking on another story. This is a great way to start your publicity efforts and making yourself relevant. If you can, start with newsjacking on an existing story. Stating in your lead-off paragraph that you read said article and shared it with your followers (link to where you shared it so the journalist can see that you actually did it) is an excellent way to grab attention. If there are any comments on your share, reply to them.

Then tell the journalist that you have a follow up angle that adds something to what they just wrote, or you have an angle that goes against what they just wrote and offers the other side. In one sentence (yes, one) state what your angle is.

Pitch Email Type 3

For when you followed the advice given in an article you've read in the publication or heard on the show Journos and editors love follow-up stories

Hi Emily,

So, I followed the advice of the meditation expert you interviewed last month and thought you might be interested in a follow-up story.

For 20 minutes, twice a day, I meditated. And I kept a diary of how I felt and how much clearer my thoughts were, and my work productivity levels soared.

I run the MomsInDesign company in Dublin and I am now advocating meditation for women across our membership (10,000), partnering with experts and providing assistance.

We are planning a meditation welcome party for next month (insert date and time) if you are interested in coming along. We would love to have you. We will have some of members there and they are happy to pose for photos and I have two women (links to them) who are happy to be interviewed.

Pretty excited to be offering this to our members!

Sandra

Element 1 - Lead off: This first paragraph highlights clearly that you follow the journalist's writings. Already you are in!

Element 2 – what you want the journalist to do: You are now advocating it to more women, and you want the journalist to know that their article has had a huge spin-off impact.

Element 3 - Newsworthiness: You are planning an event that you would like them to come to. You can put a date in here too. This email offers the reporter a lot of time to consider if they want to attend.

Element 4 - Sign off and a little extra: A meditation party is something a little different! Ending on an excited note exudes enthusiasm.

Why this one works

This is a really clever way of getting noticed. I worked in media organisations for 17 years and I know that many say they've read my articles but actually haven't. I know this because of what they say about the article. But this clearly highlights that you have read it and followed it, even better! You are positioning yourself as a reader but also as someone who is pitching a story.

Follow-on stories were a major thing during my time in newsrooms and still are. And often follow-ons fell through the cracks because another story comes along, or a major event happens and the good intention of following up goes out the window. Here you have done the work of offering all the elements for a follow-on piece. Journalists and editors will love you for this and you'll get noticed by having put the effort in. State you are available to be interviewed and/or that you are happy for them to share your story with their followers on social media or as a story in their edition. You might get to write a guest post and even get a byline - how cool is that! This type of story often runs as a guest type post. These are a great way of getting publicity.

Pitch Email Type 4

Position yourself as the expert: For when you want to share your expertise through your writing, a video or audio (just one)

Hi Kevin,

I am a former banking expert who would like to propose an idea for an article that would make an interesting piece for the newspaper's business profile section or for your online blog.

In 2015, I left my CEO job at a banking firm and set off to cycle around Ireland with no phone! During this time, I came up with two business ideas that I am now turning into a reality. One of which is a credit card online insurance safety check for business owners.

I'd like to write a piece emphasising the need for time and space away to facilitate idea creation. This space has allowed me time to create ideas, one of which has secured funding capital of 500,000 euro.

I want to share what I learned on my cycle around the roads of Ireland!

I have photos too.

Mark

PS: Here is a list of other publications I've written for: List here and links to a website, blog about the cycle or video diary.

Element 1 - Lead off: You are positioning yourself as an expert by stating clearly you have ideas of interest.

Element 2 – what do you want the journalist to do: Your CTA here is to get the journalist to know you better. They don't have to click a link each time, this time you are giving them a short snippet of you.

Element 3 - Newsworthiness: A turnaround story. You left banking, went on a cycle around Ireland with no phone but returned to banking albeit with new ideas. This story is a great example of showing expertise and personality.

Element 4 - Sign off and a little extra: This is a feel-good sign-off and gives the impression that your article will also be feel good. A journalist will be keen to see some photos too.

Why this one works

I only recommend this if you have time to write quality articles, make engaging videos or audio. Don't try this if you are starting off from scratch as this will eat into your time and resentment will build up if it impinges too much on your time and in the end, it doesn't get published. You won't deliver a good article. And your relationship with said journalist won't get off to a good start.

You can position yourself as the expert without pitching an article too, of course. So don't feel the need to pitch your writing chops especially when you don't feel confident about them. You can easily switch this template to stating that you think your story about taking a time out would be of interest to readers of a certain section or would be of interest because it has made news headlines recently. The context speaks for itself here because the writer has firmly placed himself as an authority in this field.

This is also a good example of not being afraid to put some of your personal life into your pitch. A journalist will be instantly asking why this person decided to leave their high-powered CEO job to cycle around Ireland. Journalists like some intrigue but also like to see a bit of the person behind the story. In this case, they will want to find out more.

Pitch Email Type 5

For when you want to invite the journalist to your event

PRO TIP: If the journalist can't make it, ask in a follow-up email if it is possible that a photographer could attend.

Hi Emily,

Being a follower of your writing, I have discovered useful tips on how to run my business. Your support of start-ups in particular is something myself and other moms really appreciate. Your regular spotlight on new businesses is helping all of us.

I run MomsInDesign (link), and we are setting up a stall at xx market at xx time on xx date. We will have moms there who run 6-figure businesses and who now want to give back and provide free one-on-ones to other moms (link to moms).

Pretty fantastic, right?

I thought you might be interested, and we wanted to reach out to you because you have been an inspiration to us through your writing.

Hope you can come along.

If not, let us know if we can be of help.

Sandra

Element 1 - Lead off: Be careful not to sound too eager. This tone strikes a good chord.

Element 2 – What you want the journalist to do/know: Your CTA here is to get the journalist to your event. Give them lots of time to decide (at least a month) and share what will happen. A link to the event is good to include.

Element 3 - Newsworthiness: Ideally, you would like them to do a preview and to come along. Moms giving other moms advice on how to run a business is a newsworthy angle.

Element 4 - Sign off and a little extra: Getting a journalist to leave their desk is hard. If Emily is seeking out new stories and journalists always are, then this will be an event she would hope to attend if her schedule allows.

Why this one works

Journalists are under crazy pressure all the time. From meetings to writing social media content to conducting interviews to planning and writing the stories. It is a non-stop wheel. Getting a journalist to leave their desk and go to an event is a mammoth task. Especially if you are pitching to national outlets. As a journalist, I didn't like having a lot of events to go to in my week because I knew when I came back my workload was going to be immense. No one covers for the journalist when they are out. The work is there and ready for them when they return and the deadline looms. So being out of the office at an event won't be decided upon lightly.

If they do come, remember that and deal with them with this in mind. Keeping them waiting or not providing what you said you were going to provide are sure fire ways of burning bridges. I wouldn't pitch for every event that you have. **Be picky and send in a pitch for your best events; the ones that provide the most value**. Local outlets in particular like to get photos from events like this, as a page of photos from this will be a talking point in the next issue.

If you feel that the journalist isn't interested in coming along, then pitch something from the event itself, a speaker, a stand, a product, or service. Get more specific if the event itself isn't enough. That way you will get them to do a preview at the very least. Also, let the journalist know in your follow-up email that you will have someone taking photos and can send in some afterwards. Local outlets are always interested in photos from events.

Pitch Email Type 6

The Follow up email: For when you want to follow-up on a previous email (Don't be afraid to ask if they got your first email but being overly pushy is a turn-off. Always include your original email.)

Follow up - Re: MomsInDesign Meditation Party

Hi Emily,

I just wanted to follow up because I know it has been a busy time with (name a story that you've seen everywhere) and things get lost sometimes.

We recently held an event for our MomsInDesign group, and we had over 800 moms attend. We had some amazing speakers including Melinda Bazenstoke who spoke about her battle with depression as a mother and after years working in marketing, decided to change roles and work with mothers instead.

Amazing hey?

Melinda, who is a bestselling author and speaker is available for interview. I can also forward you her speech as background if you like. I think her story might be of interest to the many female business owners who read the business section.

Happy to provide more details and some photos from the event.

Sandra

Element 1 - Lead off: Make sure you forward the previous email and put "Follow up" in the subject line, so they know it is about something you sent before. This makes them not want to miss out on something that they didn't pay attention to the first time.

Element 2 – What you want the journalist to do: The event has already happened, but you can still get publicity after the event. You want the journalist to interview Melinda.

Element 3 - Newsworthiness: You explain why she is someone worth interviewing and why you think she suits what the journalist does.

Element 4 - Sign off and a little extra: It is always good to offer more details in a follow-up pitch email. Because maybe there was some detail that they wanted but forgot to ask you. Here, you are reminding them that you can provide more.

Why this one works

Following up on a story proves to the journalist that you proudly stand over it and feel it worth their while to take another look at it. Many don't follow up and take the no response as a rejection. Things do get lost, forgotten, or are flagged for a future date. By not following up, you sit on the other side of your email wondering and ruminating on whether or not it will get covered. If your story is timely and you feel it should be used, then follow up with an email. It certainly doesn't hurt.

I recommend calling when your story is about to go stale, and you want to know either way. Take a look at Chapter 6 where I've gone into detail about when you should and shouldn't call. I recommend emailing at least one week after you've sent your first email. This also depends on the timeframe you have given yourself to get your story covered. The more time you give yourself the better because you may need to spend a lot of time following up.

I always call the week before my pitch goes stale. I have a short script ready with my four pointers (as in the email I sent) and I get ready to either speak directly to the journalist or leave a message. Don't not leave a message. Sometimes and especially when coming up to a deadline, a journalist will not answer the phone to outside numbers. They will get the message later. Unless it is someone they need to talk to. By not leaving a message, you are missing out on your opportunity. And always remind them of your email, your story, and your number for them to call back. But pick your calls wisely and I recommend you read my section about this in Chapter 5 before deciding what to do.

Pitch Email Type 7 - The Thank You email

For when you want to thank the reporter but also mention anything else that could be helpful to them in the future.

Hi Emily,

I very much appreciate you including us in this week's issue/show/episode etc. (Insert details here.) We are happily sharing it on our social media and so far, it has gotten some great reaction (insert link here to where you shared).

We know there are women who would like to start a business but are afraid of the costs of childcare, if their idea is good enough or where to start.

We are putting together a day of free online power hours for Cyber Monday. We are asking women to donate what they can as part of a fee, and we will put it towards a future event.

Thought it might be of interest. For now, we want to thank you and maybe this story might be of interest to you in the future.

Best wishes, Sandra

Element 1 - Lead off: You have a relationship with the journalist and thanking them is important to keep the conversation going. Also, you never know what kind of pressure the journalist was under to get your story done.

Element 2 – What you want the journalist to do Your CTA here is actually nothing urgent, so this is refreshing. You are taking the time to appreciate the publicity you got and to start a conversation with the journalist without having an agenda.

Element 3 - Newsworthiness: A second event is mentioned here and if the two events are close together, the journalist may not be eager to feature you twice so closely. Which is why a content calendar for media pitches is vital! But there is no harm in mentioning the second event so long as it isn't too close to the first one.

Element 4 - Sign off and a little extra: This is a feel-good sign-off and shows you appreciate the coverage. Which is something that is rarely done.

Why this one works

Being thankful opens up many doors. When a journalist features you, you must remember all the others that didn't get featured. Show gratitude because it takes a lot of effort to put a story together under immense pressure and to a deadline. Yes, journalists are used to deadlines, but they are not often told "thank you". Thank you also keeps the door open and if you have built up a good relationship, you can use this template to mention another story.

BUT DON'T PITCH IT HARD RIGHT NOW. Mention it for another time and if the journalist wants more, they will ask. Don't come across as disingenuous by pitching a story disguised as a thank you. There is a careful line here and be mindful of it.

Three Final Email Types

For when a journalist leaves for another job or retires

For when you are responding to a callout and

For when you see a call for pitches online

I'm firstly going to deal with the email you could send a journalist when he/she **decides it is time to move on to another publication or retire**. Building a relationship with anyone takes time, trust, and connection. Journalists value these qualities hugely in people and especially those who they have grown to know. So, when you get an email from a journalist letting you know that they are moving on, you should take the time to craft a meaningful response. This journalist has invested their time and energy into writing stories about you that have helped you to grow more awareness for your business. You have provided the story content and of course that is important too.

Valuing relationships and connection is an important consideration in media publicity. Just because this journalist is moving on doesn't mean that he/she won't be knocking on your door for a story in the future. They may be at a major national outlet and need a good source. Respond to this email by wishing them well and hoping to carry on the conversation with them in their new role.

If they are retiring, then you could offer to buy them lunch sometime to have a friendly chat away from the context of the media. Send a card to him/her, post a thank you on social media. Showing your appreciation is really important. Also be mindful that when a person leaves, there is always a handover period. If you have been a reliable contact, then you will most likely be one of the people that will be mentioned to the new journalist. This saves you time and energy building a connection with the new journalist. Getting a recommendation from another journalist about a good contact is always given a lot of weight by the new one.

When you know a new journalist is starting, this is a great time to pop into their inbox and say hi and introduce yourself. Let them know a little about you and how you can help them. Mention anything you've done for the previous journalist and end the email by welcoming them. There is no need to send in a pitch, unless you know they are looking for stories. They will most likely have a lot on their plate as with anyone with a new job. Reaching out and making that connection early is a good idea because they may be in dire need of stories if they are finding it difficult to get started.

Responding to a Callout

You see a callout from a journalist on Twitter under the hashtag #journorequest and you want to respond (Note, check this hashtag often for journalists looking for stories). Or you have signed up to HARO (Help A Reporter Out) and you want to respond to one of the requests for comments. Being active on Twitter (also, look for #prrequest) is a vital first step and when you see a callout either on the social media platform or elsewhere on HARO for example, the most important thing you need to be able to do is ACT FAST. Below is how I suggest you construct your email.

Subject Line: State what the callout is.

For example: Twitter callout for experts in home schooling: I homeschool 3 under 10! or

HARO request: Home schooling made easier with a 7-step guide

Be direct and succinct in your communication. Often when journalists post on Twitter or HARO they are:

- Looking to put an article together under pressure and need responses really quickly

- A breaking news story needs to be developed and they want commentary

- A journalist is finding it difficult to get sources for their story and needs to cast the net wider.

You need to be quick and remember that journalists will be receiving lots of responses, so you need to offer value. If it is a callout on Twitter, comment on the post letting the journalist know that you will be sending on a response. And within minutes of writing this tweet, you need to have that response in their inbox.

Make sure you follow the instructions. See what way the journalist wants to receive the information. They might want a quick comment on Twitter or will send on questions via email for you to answer. In the case of HARO, you will get an email to respond to that will no longer work once the deadline has passed.

Answer the questions that are included in the callout and try to add something unique and different that offers another insight. This gives you a better chance of being chosen for the article. Keep your email short and always include a bio with links. Make it easy for the journalist to spot the gems in your response. If it gets used, be sure to share it and tag the outlet to thank them. Read on below to get help on getting clearer with your first line or as what I call it your one-liner.

Your one-liner

Yes! This is the one line that describes you. This line states clearly what you do and how you help. This can change depending on each pitch as you may want to place emphasis on a particular skillset that suits your pitch best.

Examples:

1. I am a mental health expert who helps couples cope with the fallout from divorce and what they need to achieve to live a happy life again. - *okay, but long winded.*

2. I'm a lawyer and the founder of Delightful Divorce, a service that helps couples overcome the pain and anxiety around marriage breakdown. I'm also an expert in alternative medicine and on my blog, I talk a lot about the various treatments that have changed so many lives. - *This is confusing and not focused.* Also, when using the name of your company, think about whether a journalist would be familiar with it. There isn't any point using it if the journalist has never heard of it before. Even though I do find this one intriguing.

3. I am a mental health expert who helps divorcees - *good.* In the next sentence, you can then go on to mention Delightful Divorce and how it helps. But keep these details really short, like one line is enough.

Subject lines

As a former journalist and editor, I'm not into hyped subject lines. There are so many of those nowadays that for me at least I instantly delete them. Nothing annoyed me more than to get a subject line with BREAKING NEWS in capitals and inside there is nothing breaking about it, it is a story about a launch of a book next month. Subject lines with "live the life of your dreams", "would you believe this just happened" or "OMG, you have to open this right now". I instantly deleted these.

Don't put press release in there or pitch, the journalist knows you are about to do that. Use this space wisely. Tell the journalist clearly what your story is. Over 30% of emails are opened based on a good subject line (Cision Media). Places to get inspiration for writing good subject lines include popular magazines. I encourage you to pick up magazines and study their headlines. They are a great place to learn how to put together a captivating headline.

Use the active voice:

- YouTuber gives top 10 tips to work better on camera
- Make-up company signs Beauty Influencer for new docuseries
- Brighton actress lands a role in Netflix original fly-on-the-wall series that focuses on therapy for couples

PRO TIP: Don't use words like awesome, must-see, fantastic. You can't be sure that this is the case, and it makes you look more involved that you should be when pitching. Stay more neutral and newsier. Don't be overly descriptive because a headline gets to the point, the description comes later - in the body of your email. Influencer signs deal with new hot show OR Amazing company to give designers a chance to work at Dior. How do you know if the show is hot, or the company is amazing? Keep these words out.

Closing lines

Try to write something that leaves an impression, asks a question, or expresses emotion. Signoffs don't have to be just "Yours sincerely". Move away from formality and try one of these 20.

1. Thanks for being an inspiration to...

2. You're an inspiration to our group

3. Thanks for considering it

4. Hope to finally meet you (event pitch email)

5. I appreciate everything you have done for us and for our sector. We so enjoyed working with you (for a journalist that is leaving or retiring)

6. With very best wishes for your day

7. Hope this helps (for follow-on emails)

8. Look forward to your next story (You are going to read it despite it not being about you)

9. These people (insert sector) need support right now

10. Let me know what you think

11. Need anything else? Let me know.

12. Look forward to reading your coverage on (major story coming up, election, for example)

13. Considering this story means a lot to us

14. Thanks for reading this email

15. Hope this week's issue/program/show goes well. I know these are crazy times right now.

16. Thanks for including us in your piece

17. Have a good day

18. Need me to set up an interview?

19. Sending good vibes for your week/weekend

20. Admire your work.

CHAPTER 15

PHOTOGRAPHS

Photographs alone are one of the best ways to secure coverage. In the local publicity scene, good photos are gold, and receiving ones that leap from the page is rare. This is not so much the case in the bigger organisations, as they receive photos from a wider variety of sources, all vying for national recognition like freelancers, as well as amateur and professional photographers, the nature enthusiast. And also factor in their own photographers who cover a lot of events so they can find a great photo worthy of a front or back page or any of the prime pages inside.

While being a good writer is important when it comes to writing your press release and/or pitch email, photos can reflect your personality and showcase your organisation in a unique way. In this chapter, I will relay my experiences working with press photographers and freelancers both amateur and professional. I will focus on what a photocall is, how to organise photoshoots, and show you how to be ready to make the most of the opportunity once your photos get published.

Photocalls

A photocall is a short notice letting members of the press know that you have a photo opportunity for them. It is much shorter than a press release and a pitch email, and it details the who, what, where, when and some of the why. It can be a launch event, the announcement of a new signing, an unveiling of a mural, the dedication of a bench, etc. Photocalls don't have to be things that happen on a large scale. They can be inside your business, like the handing over of a substantial cheque to a charity. If you are going to include props of any kind, such as hiring a character in costume, or have staff or a spokesperson perform or wear a certain colour, mention that in your photocall.

Example photocall notice

PHOTOCALL

You are invited to attend a photocall for the launch of the {fill in details here}
Date: 20 January 2019 Time: 12 noon
Where: At the James Joyce statue on Willow Road, Dublin 4 {fill in full details here, include postcode}

TV soap star James Hodderington will be launching the product (details here) and will be available for short interviews afterward.

He will talk about his hopes for 2019 after what he calls "2018, the year I realised I needed to change".
You are welcome to attend and to ask questions.

ENDS

For more information, contact Sandra on {fill in number here that you are contactable at and an email address that is checked regularly} We will be playing James's favourite tunes. His playlist, he tells us, has some Eminem classics on there! We hope he "loses himself in the moment!" He has also promised to sign autographs after.

The information in the paragraph above goes after ENDS. Everything above ends is information you are happy for the public to know. Send this photocall notice via individual emails to each press photographer in each news outlet you are targeting and to the editor in each. Because it states that he is available for interviews, the editor may want to send a journalist as well as a photographer. In the email, try to state something you like about their work (the press photographer) or a photo you've seen in the newspaper/magazine by way of an introduction to what you are sending them (the two don't have to be connected in any way). It is not necessary to do this for all the emails, but for those people you really want to turn up, you should make a special effort to get them there.

By mentioning that the special guest James is available for autographs afterward, this puts into a photographer's mind the idea that many of his fans will show up and that there will be chances to get photos with members of the public. These photos can light up a news page, especially if his fans are absolutely crazy about him. Photographers will be thinking of the main shots and also of some social and candid shots that they can capture.

PRO TIP: Just like journalists are on the look-out for stories, press photographers are always on the look-out for photos that they can send to the nationals. By getting them there and setting something up that is interesting, you are increasing your chances that the photographer may get something worthy of a national newspaper or magazine. They will already have contacts in this area and will do the pitching for you. How great is that!

Hire your own photographer

Photocalls are a way of letting a publication know that you have a photo opportunity that you think is worth them taking the time to come over and take. But don't rely solely on them. If you are struggling to get responses or are only starting to build relationships, then you will need to hire your own. You will want to have your own record of the event too and have your own photos taken. For many journalists, particularly during the economic boom, photocalls were hugely popular and often involved scantily clad models posing with a sign or with a person, sitting in or on a car and so on. You get the picture. And oftentimes, these images landed on pages 3 or 5 and gained the attention the business desired. This is just one aspect of photocalls that you may be familiar with.

However, photocalls have changed a lot over the years and instead of just being about having an eye-catching image, they are more about storytelling and capturing a moment that reveals something about humankind. Their value as a publicity tool has increased so much more since social media. They are a valuable tool to use in any aspect of your business when you want to attract attention and they are simple to put together. Photocalls can sell your business or product if you put some imagination into them. I'm not saying get a scantily clad model to help you but thinking about ways to brighten up your photo opportunity really helps an editor or press photographer decide whether or not it is worth their time.

Make it interesting

Picture how you would like the photocall location to look and work back listing out the things you need to put in place to construct that image. Keep it simple for your first one but do try to add a little something to it to make it more interesting. This is where your knowledge of the particular outlet you are pitching to will be especially useful.

- Think about whether there is an interesting location you can get the photo taken in
- Is there a particularly good time of the day or night to get it done? Are you better off taking it inside, or would you benefit more from an outdoor shot?
- How many people will be in the photo?
- For groups, between 3 and 5 is ideal. But if there is more, it is all about how to construct the image and how it looks so don't limit yourself but don't have an overcrowded photo either.
- Are there certain people who need to be in it, and are they willing to move out of their comfort zone and say go to the local park or an amusement park if this was required?
- For example, if you are involved in building a playground for your community, would your CEO go down a slide or dress up for the launch?
- Do you want to ask people to wear a certain colour or a certain top/hat/scarf? These are just a few parameters that you need to think of before you plan the shoot. If you are looking at adding outfits into the mix, you'll need to factor in time to get them and to make sure they fit.

If you are hoping to get coverage in a tabloid, then you need to think of what type of pictures they use in their issue. You can only get this by looking at several issues. The same goes for broadsheets. And if you haven't guessed by now, the type of photo each of these outlets prefers is vastly different. A press photographer will instinctively know what works in each.

You can take them yourself but...

Yes, of course you can take them yourself but remember there are certain skills required when taking press photos. Some you will know and some you won't. I'm not a professional photographer so I'm not going to go into that here. If you feel you have the knowledge and expertise, then by all means try. If it is a major event, it would be wise to get expert help in. Let your first event as a photographer be something with less pressure attached. You can learn by observing and reviewing what photos were taken and what got printed. When all things are considered, I believe that hiring a photographer with press experience is an invaluable and crucial move. They have skills that only they can have because they have inside knowledge of what works.

Your options:

- Invite along press photographers working in publications in your locality
- Hire a freelance press photographer

Firstly, they come from a press background and will have insider knowledge that you just couldn't possibly have or acquire. A press photographer is a professional who knows what will and won't get used in a newspaper or magazine. This information is invaluable and benefitting from it first-hand from one of these photographers will serve you well in your first and subsequent photocalls. And also, there is the added benefit of building a relationship with someone who knows the press. You can invite press photographers along and they hopefully will come get the photo that works for them and submit it for consideration to the editor and submit others to various other publications that they feel may like particular images. You won't get to build any significant connections at the photocall itself because press photographers are always looking to the next job, and they are under pressure to get photos that are newsworthy. However, they now know you and if you've set up a memorable photo opportunity, they will remember that the next time you ask them to come along. Remember, your attention will be dragged in numerous directions, and photographers will know instantly if they have something they can use. They will want to get it and leave to send the photo in and to move on to the next job. You actually might not get talking to the photographers at all. But don't let that disappoint you.

To make this a lot easier and take the uncertainty out of it all, you can hire a freelance press photographer who will have the connections to speed up the journey your photo will take to get into the right hands. Hiring one prevents you from being at the mercy of a major event happening and a newspaper photographer having to change their mind at the last minute. A lot of press photographers working for publications may be prevented from doing commercial work if they are full time with a media outlet and they cannot compromise the organisation. But there are others who are freelance and will do it once they weigh up all the pros and cons of doing the shoot. So, ask around and get to know the ones you can try to hire.

Think long-term

Hiring a photographer is a worthwhile expense if you are thinking long-term. You will start building a relationship with this photographer and they can be your go-to person in terms of getting photos taken that media outlets prefer to receive. Be careful not to come across as someone whose primary reason for hiring them/inviting them is to get insider knowledge. This won't work. Many photographs bat that off with "I'm just the photographer, I don't have any say in the stories". And most of the time they don't, but photographers are out and about more often than journalists, and they hear stories, they see people, they talk to people. They will pass on stories to journalists if they feel they are worth mentioning. Building a friendship is especially important. This friendship can be built by just inviting them to the launch or hiring them for it. If there is a photographer you admire, it would be wise to hire them. But also invite others so you get the best chance of featuring in as many outlets as possible.

Don't forget online channels and sharing your experience

Also, don't forget your online presence. Get photos that you can use across your online channels and you should try to get some video content. I suggest 3 short videos capturing the preparation/behind the scenes, the event, and the aftermath. Talk about your preparation, how you're feeling, things you've learned, mistakes made, how you managed to get photographers to it, and what you hope will happen as a result of your photocall. It is a good way to get the attention of your followers by showing them inside your business. It is also an excellent way to warm up a cold audience by letting them see how you are trying to get publicity and allowing them to follow your journey.

Indoor vs outdoor

This is an important aspect that you need to decide on early because it will influence everything that comes after. For your first photocall, it is probably best to stay indoors. That way, you have more control over the environment you are in and you can "set things up" without having the public watch and ask a million questions and offer their advice. Doing it outdoors on a busy street is a good way of getting extra attention, especially if you are taking over a particular corner of a busy street or shopping mall. If you do decide to go outdoors, have a sign explaining what is happening. Have a link for people to go to if they want to find out more. Have it visually striking and interesting enough for people to want to take a selfie at it or post a photo to social media.

Remember too that if you are doing it outside and want to attract some attention that you can let people know via your press release and on social media that they are welcome to come along and join in the activity. You may not like to do this if you have a major celebrity as they will attract enough passing attention, but it is worth considering if you want to build momentum in advance. People are always attracted to crowds and want to know what is happening. So, having some people there will attract more.

Caught in the moment

For a press photographer, capturing a caught in the moment type of photo is gold. They know that these are the ones that will catch the eye of an editor. A good photographer will always be on the lookout for one of these. However, these don't always happen, and they aren't ones that can be staged easily or at all. So, having members of the public present can help add a different dimension. You could ask the photographer you've hired to set up some photos with members. These can often serve as a funny or "caught in a moment" type of shot. A good press photographer will recognise that another moment which is more important may emerge from this scenario and will do their best to get the best image.

Example: At a dog charity event to which I invited a press photographer via a photocall, a 99-year-old woman was in attendance. She agreed to be in a photo. The woman had a dog of her own that had recently passed away. The photographer asked the woman if she wouldn't mind posing with the celebrity, who she was a big fan of, and the photographer caught a beautiful moment between the two, where the celebrity comforted her on the loss of her dog. The photo made a page three tabloid with a short news story about the old woman and a bit about her background.

This story was then followed up by a television programme looking for people older than 100 who remembered World War 2 and what it was like to live in those times. This happened because a press photographer was keeping an eye on the whole surrounds of the photo, not just what was set up in front of him. Now, this doesn't happen every day, but you would be surprised at how often it can happen.

This is why picking a good photographer is such an important decision. It pays to do your research and hire a press photographer whose work you like. Get to know their work as much as possible and try to meet them for a coffee before your shoot. In this conversation, it is important to listen and figure out what will work best for both you and the photo opportunity. You need to figure out if what you had envisioned matches with or comes close to what the photographer is thinking. Listen to the photographer and go back to your ideas and rework them. You can, of course, try both your ideas and the photographer's, but press photographers can be more expensive than regular photographers, so be aware of your budget beforehand.

Make the area interesting to photograph

Don't expect magic from the photographer if your setting and background are bland. Give the photographer something to work with. If you are doing blog posts or short videos leading up to your photocall, get suggestions from people online and from those involved in the shoot on what props to use. This is a good way to get their interest and involvement beforehand and they will be more invested in getting the best photos. You can get advice and support from outside your circle by asking in photography Facebook groups.

Photo captions

You need to make sure that all photos are captioned correctly with the names of the people and also in the file information section. Your photographer should be doing this, as this is what you are hiring him/her to do. But if you feel the job could be done by you or someone else then you could suggest taking over and getting the captions if the photographer seems to be too busy. You should check all captions before the people in the photo disperse. And always check them before they are submitted to any publication.

A previous publication I worked in received several photos, some of which were uncaptioned, except for one which read: "Caption? Where is the f**king caption??????" The frustrated sub-editor placed it on a page and left it like that to be filled in later. Unfortunately, or hilariously if you prefer, it was printed. Needless to say, the people in the photo were not happy with this caption running under their photo. So, make sure that captions are included for all photos, even if a series of photos involves the same people in the same spot with different expressions on their faces. They need to be named.

What a caption includes

- First and second names of everyone.
- Their titles, if needed.
- Where they are from (approximately).
- At what event.
- Where the event was held.
- Why the event happened.
- When the photo was taken.
- Anything interesting in the photo.
- Any titles of anything like books, artwork, a sculpture.
- A Call to Action, if necessary (an event coming up or a launch).
- Who took the photo, their name and what organisation they are with. Mention if there is any embargo on the photo and/or if it is an exclusive

Think about variety

Be sure to get a range of photos. Have a look in mind that you would like and be open to others. Do you want people looking straight to the camera? Do you want some of them looking straight to the camera and others looking away? Do you want to catch a moment? The latter is always great if it is possible to get such photos. But remember, some sections in news outlets want a straight-up professional photo with no gimmicks or props, so be sure to get a range with props and a range without. If you are working with people who have no experience of a photocall or having their photo taken for publication, it is wise to speak to them beforehand and make them aware of what you want to achieve.

There is nothing worse than having a location all set up, props ready but the people holding them looking like they would prefer to be anywhere else except where you have put them. This is a disaster, and even the best press photographer cannot do much about this. So, prep them and let them know the vibe of the shoot, what you are aiming for, and what publications are interested in covering it. You should have a good idea of the latter by receiving replies from your photocall notice. Also, think about where people stand. "Don't line them up in a row and shoot them." This is a phrase in the photojournalism world when people are lined up against a walk, they stand straight with their backs to the wall and the photo is taken. Please stay away from this. If you need to photograph a group of people, have some of them sit, have some stand, have them turn their bodies slightly so they are not facing the camera head-on, have them looking and feeling comfortable. Try to talk to them a little bit and help them to forget that the camera is there. Then start the shoot.

If people are feeling uncomfortable, you can give them props to hold that are relevant. If it is a brochure, they can be reading it or showing it to the person beside them. Feel free to tell them if you think their hair is messy or their make-up needs fixing. They will thank you, trust me. I had my photo taken once, and one side of my hair was sticking out. I wished someone had told me. I looked like I just got out of bed! Not my favourite look, even in my student days. The next time, I brought a small mirror and checked everything. Needless to say, the photo was a whole lot better.

What to wear

This is a major topic of conversation in relation to photocalls and rightly so. Talk to those getting their photo taken in advance and ask them not to wear anything with a busy pattern or with a logo (unless it is your company logo). Get them to pick neutral colours. Have a look in mind and ask them to adhere to it. Now, don't have everyone in black or navy suits; that would just be plain boring. Ask them to wear colours that suit them, clothes they have worn before, not something they are wearing for the first time. I guarantee you; they will look uncomfortable if they wear a skirt that is too tight or shoes that haven't been worn in. Let the participants know if you will be travelling anywhere for the shoot – for example, to the local running track or park. This has a bearing on the amount of time they will need to set aside for the shoot. It will also let them know if they need to wear a comfy pair of shoes to walk over to the location or if they need to bring a rain jacket. There is nothing worse than turning up for what you thought was going to be a quick headshot and then to be told that you are being brought to a park five miles away. Respect their time and they will respect what you are trying to do at the photocall.

Some other things to think about before the photoshoot:

From my experience with photographers, you need to give him/her space to do their job. Yes, you are entitled to help and guide them to get the photo you want. But, if they are being invited there and you are not paying them, they are entitled to take whatever photo they see are the best ones. Also, if they see something better or want to try something else, let them. Trust that they are seeing something newsworthy. Let their fresh eyes and creativity influence the shoot.

Always, always look at the background of your photo. Is there anything sticking up out of someone's head, for example, such as a long branch from a tree. Are there slogans? If someone covers a part of the slogan, what words or letters are left? If the word "Titanic" is part of your company name, for example, you don't want the last four letters to be obscured! Always, always look at any tags or writing on people's clothes. Don't be afraid to ask them to change, or better still, ask them to wear clothing without any writing. Do you want a very clean-cut type of photoshoot, or do you prefer it to be colourful? This is where you need to think ahead and decide are these images just for this photoshoot or do you plan to use them as part of future campaigns?

Ask yourself if you want to incorporate your brand colours heavily into the shoot. Your brand colours should be part of the image anyway, but how much you want this to be a part of the photos is something you need to give serious consideration to. Do you want the photos to be very commercial, or do you want them to tell a story instead? A press photographer will want a story. You may want both. My advice would be to look at photoshoots that other businesses in your area have done and take inspiration from them. Get to know what you like and what you don't like. Do you want close-up shots of staff to show their teeth or not? (you may be surprised or not happy with what you see if you get them to smile with their teeth!!) Use furniture wisely. You could try using a desk and placing people around it in an interesting way. Your photographer should be able to help you with this, telling you what will work and what won't. Be ready to take on board their suggestions.

Direction and collaboration on the photoshoot

Always, always be in the driver's seat at the photoshoot and wear the organiser's hat on the day. You will have a lot more leeway with this when you are paying for a photoshoot but even when not, press photographers from a publication will appreciate that someone is in control. They are used to arriving at photoshoots that are lacking organization so be the exception.

For invited photographers, you can by all means make suggestions, but don't be overbearing, as this is not welcomed, and will most likely kill off any relationship with that photographer before you get the chance to know him/her. It is also good for your commercial photos to let the photographer have some kind of input into the composition. It is best for this to be a collaborative effort. The results will be much better if you try to work together. The photographer knows the difference instantly between a commercial and news photo, so don't be worried. If you have studied their work for a while, you'll have confidence knowing that they are good at what they do.

People involved in the photocall feel more comfortable if the shoot is directed and there is a structure or a plan of action. There is nothing worse than when people feel like the shoot isn't properly organised and they are left standing around wondering what is happening next. If they are colleagues, try to pick a day and time that suits them best to do the shoot so that you get their best attention. If you are paying models or others to be there, you need to work them into your shoot.

Prior to the photocall/photoshoot, it is wise to send around the plan for the allocated time in advance of the shoot itself. When people feel they are waiting or hanging around, they start to become complacent about your shoot, and they tend to become less dedicated. You need them to be dedicated to creating the best photos possible. Photocalls are notorious for running over so stick to a timetable and be the one that hurries things up if you feel there is a need to.

Think about the atmosphere you want to create at your photoshoot. Do you want a fun atmosphere or a more serious one? This will impact how people react, and this will come across in the photos. You could consider having music playing at your shoot. Are you going to have Jay Z or Mozart? Your type of music will impact the atmosphere on the shoot. People react to music, and you should choose this wisely.

Plan and think ahead

Issue your photocall notice two to three weeks before your photocall date for locals and up to four months ahead for national publications. This gives ample time for editors and photographers to mark it into their diary and to plan other engagements around. Also, send a reminder to both four to five days prior just in case they have forgotten or not marked it in. I would send another one a couple of weeks in advance to the national publications. Include any extra things you have added to the photocall, as this may help change their mind about going if they had previously decided that they were not going to cover it. Include the original photocall notice in your reminder emails. When planning out your photocall, try to think of it as the future image of your business and what you want to portray.

After the photocall

If you have hired your own photographer, he/she will send you all the photos, and it will be up to you to send them on to the press. They may also offer to send a couple to press outlets if they have connections but depending on your agreement, they may not be obliged to do so. If you find yourself sending them to the press, it can be very time-consuming, and I suggest that you have this in your agreement with the photographer you hire that they organise all the photos into groupings and have them captioned properly.

To save time and headaches, put your photos into sets. Label the sets according to your publicity plan. Label them with phrases like "inside shots of", "outside shots of", "group shots", individual shots", "press shots of", "shots taken at", and so on. This will save you time when a journalist asks you for a particular type of shot, so you can quickly see if you have it. They may want a headshot of someone or another type of outside shot. Looking through 100 shots that have no titles is not something you want to be doing on a deadline. Have them labelled, and this will save you a lot of time and heartache. Have this information on the file name with more details in the File Info section of the photo's details.

Final tips

Get to know the pool of press photographers who work in your area. Their names will appear in the captions of the photos printed and online in the news outlet. A press photographer has a different range of skills to a family/wedding photographer.

Get group shots as well as headshots. Get ones with and without props. Check your background and location. It is wise to stay indoors on your first photocall. But remember, there are probably a lot more opportunities outdoors on a busy main street, and it offers more visibility to your business or product.

Don't send all the photos to every outlet. This is incredibly annoying, and no journalist will look through a batch of photos to pick from for their story. That is your job. Pick 5 to send that show variety and let them know that you have others that you can show them (Reminder: don't send them as attachments). They will ask to look at others if they need to. It is best to pick different photos to send to each outlet. Tailor them. Also, double-check the captions. Write your own captions. Remember, the photo editor may change this, but you can at least put forward your idea by writing something interesting or entertaining.

Also, check names again and again and again. Be ready for queries. Once your photos appear in the press, have your website ready, have your spokesperson ready, have your product ready and easy to find. Get a range of photos. Think about having photos taken that you can use over and over. Get some staged and some natural ones.

CHAPTER 16

THE INTERVIEW

The excitement quickly turns to nerves and a huge amount of anxiety as you realise you are unprepared for your media interview. Maybe you've never done one before, or you've done one before and it didn't go as well as you would have liked. With only a day to prepare, what do you do? When I get nervous about anything, whether in business or my personal life, I try to educate myself as much as possible. I find that the more educated I am about a problem, the less nervous I become. You have sent in your press release and now the journalist has called and wants to do a feature piece. He/she feels that an in-person interview would be best, so a feature will delve deeper into the story.

You are excited and also nervous. Or you are worried that you or your spokesperson isn't fully ready. But the interview is taking place in a few hours or tomorrow so there isn't much time. You go tell your CEO that the journalist wants to interview him/her, and he/she believes that a few minutes of preparation will suffice. In this situation, it is wise to reiterate the importance of being amply prepared for interviews. I encourage this even more so if it is a television or radio interview. Sometimes, if an interview with a newspaper journalist goes badly, you have time to correct it or to talk to the journalist about clarifying something the CEO said before the piece goes to print or goes up online. But there is nowhere to hide in a television or radio interview. It is live and everything said can't be taken back. Of course, there are prerecords but the prerecord will also be a live performance but with less pressure. Also, you'll only get a little bit of time to redo things if at all. So essentially, they are both live.

Get the full details of the interview and prepare

Firstly, look at the details you have about the interview. Does it state clearly what the interview will entail? Do you have an idea of the questions you will be asked or the area of focus, if you are part of a group story? (this is when more than one business is being interviewed for a piece in a news outlet or you are on a panel for a radio or tv show). Do you need to bring anything? What time do you need to get there? How long will you be there? Who is the interviewer? (is it the regular one or is he/she on holidays). Is there a theme to the segment? Are there any questions you need to ask beforehand? If there are, send them on right now. Are there any questions you would like to propose to them? Oftentimes, those booking podcast interviews and tv and radio researchers like to receive these well in advance as it gives them something to work from and develop.

Rehearse things like the main contributions you would like to make, based on well-researched topics and with preparation. So many things to do, I know. But the more information you have, the better you will feel. And the better your experience will be. If you feel you don't have enough information, ring that journalist/researcher/booker. Ringing will get you a quicker response and it shows that you are invested in doing a good job. You don't want to be that person that arrives and isn't prepared. This happens a lot and no matter how much journalists are prepared for this, it is still annoying and stressful, so don't do it. Be as best prepared as you can be. And be honest if you don't know something and state that you will try to get up to speed on it beforehand.

You need to know who else will be on the panel so you can see if they have been on before and what they are like. Do they typically dominate the panel, or are they more relaxed? See what the presenter is like. Are there certain things that he/she likes to talk about? You may not have a lot of time to prepare, so I suggest you look at the most recent show and take some notes.

Take a look at your wardrobe and decide right now what you will wear, and always bring a spare outfit. Having been a guest on television and worked as a researcher and planner, I've had to scramble around in the wardrobe department looking for clothing that would fit a guest who has just spilled beer all over themselves or is wearing something see-through. Have something else to wear in the car or in your bag. It will help you to relax more knowing that you have a change of clothes, should you need them. Wear a colour that flatters you. Don't wear anything too busy or hugely floral. Colours like blue, red, green, and black work well on television and for newspaper photos.

Don't wear new shoes. If you are planning to wear heels, wear ones that you've worn in and that won't make you look uncomfortable. A pair of nude or black medium-high heels are trusted by many for a reason. For guys, I suggest looking at what other guests have worn and judge your outfit based on that. Guys in particular tend to stand out more if they go with a colourful shirt or a pair of interesting socks or colourful shoes. And remember this is television and everything is visual so if you want to subtly stick out you can look at your clothes to do this. Colours like navy, purple, blue and brown are good for men. Use common sense here. Try on what you are going to wear and go look in the mirror. My best advice is to have an outfit that fits you well and that you have worn at least once before.

The interview itself

For all types of interviews, my first piece of advice here is to go with the flow. Those who don't do this come across as unnatural and even a little fake. The interview may start on a topic that isn't related to what you do but go with it and try to think on your feet. Don't pull a face because it is something daft; the presenter may be just trying to help you to relax or still has their mind on the previous guest and wants to naturally link the two together. For television and radio interviews in particular, if you get there early (and you will have to), make sure you listen to the segments that are on before you. Because the presenter may refer to these in their interview with you.

When it comes to talking about what you do, don't try to memorise your notes. Listen to the question being asked and answer it like you are telling your best friend how your day was. Don't use too much jargon and try to avoid it if you can. You may have to use some, and this is fine, but not too much. Try to come across as friendly. Smile a lot. I had one client who told me she was smiling but that she stopped once the camera was off her. She didn't realise that the camera takes longer full set shots as well as close-ups. A simple thing to forget, but remember when you are on set, you should never switch off. So, try to look relaxed and to smile when appropriate, even when the presenter is not directly talking to you. The camera may be taking a wider shot of the whole set and you are still in the shot.

Also, don't look at the camera unless you have been asked to. Look at the presenter. This is a conversation, and the viewer looking at this from their couch wants to feel like they are sitting in on a conversation, not watching a sales pitch. Don't be afraid to ask for a question to be repeated. Or if you are not quite sure what is being asked of you, it is better to know what the question is than to ramble off an answer that you think might work. It doesn't work, and you'll come across to the viewer as someone who doesn't pay attention.

Use a mirror

This is a technique that I urge you to do, no matter how difficult you may find it. And you will find it difficult the first time you do it. It is hard to do because you will notice things you don't like! But this is your chance to remedy them, so the viewer doesn't see them. Singing into a mirror is something I was taught to do when I was training to be a classical soprano singer. At every class, my teacher would ask me to sing at least one of the pieces in front of a mirror and observe things that I did facially and with my arms and legs. We would do the piece again and this time with any weird looking habits changed. Habits are hard to change so we would have to do it numerous times. But it worked every time.

When we are nervous, we have a go-to face, same with annoyance or any emotion. Be aware of what you do and how it looks. Are you speaking about something that you love but your face looks like you are telling someone their mother just died? Or the opposite, are you smiling when you are talking about something serious. Facial expressions are amplified on television. Get to know what your face looks like when you speak. You may well be surprised by what you see! Rehearse in front of the mirror before you do a tv interview. Get someone to ask you questions and answer them in front of a mirror. See how your face contorts, how your eyebrows move, or how you sometimes look angry. All of these things will come across

100-fold on television, so dealing with them beforehand is ideal. You won't get rid of these bad habits overnight, but by being aware of them, you'll remember these things when you are in the television studio. You can also record it, but I find that it is more difficult to watch yourself on video than it is to do this in front of a mirror. Will you watch the video again? Most likely, not.

Once the interview is over, thank the interviewer and the other panelists. You never know where this opportunity could lead to. Also, thank the floor staff and those who did your hair and make-up. They all have a vital role to play in helping you do a good job.

Learn from other guests and after show reaction

You get better at interviews by watching others, especially watching others that have been put in an awkward scenario or were asked a question that made them feel uncomfortable. Study how they managed this situation. Did they handle it well? And ask yourself how would you have handled it? How did you feel the presenter handled it? Did you think it was fair how the subject was brought up? And ask yourself how you would deal with any after-show reaction to a segment like this?

Also, look at the tweets that were posted from people who watched the show in real-time. What did they say about you, and is there anything on there you need to reply to? Don't be shy about learning more in this area and facing criticism from time to time. But be aware too that people can be extra critical when behind a screen and what they might say to your face is a lot different to what they post online. Take it all with a pinch of salt but try to find some constructive feedback in there. If you become good at radio and television interviews, you climb the list of media guests that are on a researcher's list. You will get asked back because you took the time to better yourself. If you have time, stay there until the show finishes (obviously out of the way of the crew) so you'll be back in the green room or watching it on a television monitor somewhere in the building.

Take notes on everything that interests you or anything you observed. Don't rely on your memory. You will forget all this on your journey home so having notes is vital. Get photos that you can use afterward on social media and promotional material. Get a photo of you with the presenters and getting make-up and hair done. You can post this up online as a way of telling your followers about your appearance on the show. And you'll also have photos you can use again.

Leave on a good note. And post a tweet or a FB post and thank the show, along with your photos. Congratulate yourself on a job well done (at home, not on social media). If you feel you didn't do as good a job as you wanted to, you can build on this experience and make sure you pitch for another show soon after, to keep your momentum going. Also, by pitching yourself closely after doing one show, you are showing any potential programmes that you have recent experience.

Attend the show beforehand if you can

In most cases, you won't have time to attend the show before your interview. Before you pitch to television shows, I recommend that you try to attend at least one. Ideally, it would be one on your list, but it doesn't have to be. It is still a huge learning experience to attend any television broadcast. Seeing the show come to life before your eyes is invaluable. Mention that you have been in the audience and mention something about the show you saw. This places you above anyone else who is blindly pitching and doesn't know a thing about what the show does and doesn't do.

Ask for a synopsis of what the segment will deal with

Television is a live medium and it is impossible to give a full outline of what will be covered. But if they are inviting you on, then it is okay to ask what angle will be taken and how you can best be prepared. You can state that you are asking because you want to be fully informed and a well-prepared guest.

Turn up earlier than you are asked to

Turn up 30 minutes before you are asked to. You just never know what is happening on live television. A guest might have got sick, and you may need to go on at a different time. Or the slot you are involved in is taking a different approach because of a breaking news story. You need to have time to prepare for any changes and to get as much information as you can. You also want to be well informed. By being there early and avoiding any rushing, you are also helping to keep your nerves in check. Use this extra time to familiarise yourself with the studio set-up and go over your notes.

Being comfortable on tv is vital

I mentioned this earlier in the chapter on photographs. But it is worth mentioning here because everything is magnified on television. You do not want to have to tug at a tight top or dress during an interview. Anything uncomfortable will start to annoy you and you will want to fix it. Wear something you have worn before. Also, don't wear anything that is see-through or that has a busy pattern. Sometimes, studios have busy backdrops, and it is best to wear a neutral colour that looks good on you. Blue, green, black, purple, red are good colours. Also, be mindful of shoes. I know of one guest who wore a great outfit but only had runners with her. She thought that the desk would cover her legs and feet. It didn't. It looked like she had neglected to pick a good pair of shoes. She didn't neglect it; she just didn't think it through fully.

Check make-up

First of all, make sure you ask if there is going to be make-up applied. That way you can turn up with a fresh face. A good moisturiser will suffice. Clean-shaven for men but this isn't always a necessity. It depends on the vibe of the show. For women if there is an eye shadow you like or you have a lipstick or lip gloss you think looks good on you, bring it along. Same for men. Make-up artists are happy to accept suggestions. And if you have to do your make-up (this happens in smaller studios sometimes) be sure to bring your own mirror to prevent shine from building up and to fix any lipstick that may have gotten on your teeth. Bringing a pocket mirror applies to men too. You may be sweating a lot and not even know. You may want make-up applied again. You may need some hair gel put on your hair that just won't lie down properly.

Go over notes

Don't be afraid to take out your notes in the green room or anywhere else in the studio. You are there as a guest and you want to give it your best. Some people see other guests and they aren't looking at notes and they feel like it would be unprofessional to go over theirs. Do what makes you feel best ahead of the interview. Taking notes and going over them is not a bad thing.

Greet presenters

Strike a rapport with the presenters. If you are all sitting in the studio waiting to go on, and if it is appropriate, ask them how their day is going, or ask how they feel the show is going so far. It is professional to come across as approachable and not just there for the sake of your job or publicity. If you are on a panel, then it is a team effort to talk about the subject in a balanced and informative way. Striking up some conversation with the presenter(s) and fellow guests is a good way to settle your nerves and to be remembered.

Vocal practice

Pick a subject in your area and start to form opinions about it and get used to hearing your voice out loud. Saying it out loud gives you an idea about how you firstly put your thoughts together and how you go on to communicate them. Don't think too hard about it at first. Just go for it. How does it sound? Do you fumble a lot over a certain word? Are there words that you find hard to say? Look out for how your face changes, what your eyes look like. Do you have any mannerisms that look weird. As you form opinions about your topics, also do your research around the same time to fact check.

Go with the flow

I mentioned this briefly earlier, but I want to go into more detail here because it is really important. Okay, so you are there to promote your business and are speaking on a topic that you know a lot about. But be aware that oftentimes the subject at hand can get the least amount of airtime. Another guest may take the topic in another direction and it is up to the presenter to bring it back. But this doesn't always happen, especially if the new subject matter is creating a storm and the presenter is told by the producer (in their headset) to let the conversation flow. It is times like this when you need to go with the flow. Listen carefully to what is being said and offer a point of view. Don't be that person who says, "But I thought this segment was about ..." (I've seen this happen). You will come across badly to the audience and those in the studio especially if one of the panelists has just revealed something deeply personal to them. Also, don't look too shocked that you never got to speak about what you were invited on to do.

Viewers remember personalities more than anything. They remember those whose personality shone through. When the segment goes off topic, this is when things get interesting. It is important to be able to adapt and remain engaged. It is the ones that can do this are those that get invited back again and again. You are there to serve the audience, first and foremost. If things go off course, you should already have asked the show's researcher to use your business name and website on your tagline for the screen. At least that way, viewers can go check out your business.

Don't try too hard to be funny

Test out your jokes on others before deciding to bring them into your content. One of the biggest mistakes people make is thinking they are funny and finding out live on air that their jokes were off point. Also know too when to drop your funny comment or joke, especially if it doesn't fit in with what is being discussed. Deliver your funny comment or joke in a natural way, not in a way that is rehearsed. You want the viewers to think you just came up with this (even though you didn't).

Be ready to react to something controversial

Be up to date on the general news stories that are happening locally and nationally. And also take a look at the major international news headlines before you go on any show. Make this a part of your preparation. This is to ensure that you are fully prepared if something controversial breaks; you will have put the time into becoming familiar with issues in your field. Be ready to state if you don't have an opinion on something. But always explain why you don't have an opinion on it, don't just say "no comment". That leaves listeners and viewers cold, and they will be turned off. "No comment" is usually used by government bodies on topics that they don't want to discuss. It is best to explain why you don't have an opinion on something. It is also okay to state that you don't have enough expertise in that area. The audience will thank you for not waffling on about something you do not know enough about.

Your social media profile

If you are pitching to be on shows, which you should start doing once you are ready, then you should keep your posts on social media up to date before you send in your pitch. If you are looking to stir up some controversy, then you will need to reflect this in your posts. There is no point in saying to the show's producer that you will stir up controversy and they go look at your social media and there are pictures of dogs dancing, or you on holidays. There is nothing there about your thoughts or opinions to suggest that you are someone who airs their views whether controversial or not. You need to fix this first and be consistent. If you are not looking to be controversial, you at least need to show that you can be good on camera or in front of an audience.

Do some videos on your social media. Show your personality outside of your business side. For lighter themed shows, you will need to have posted content that is relevant to your niche. Think of your social media as your shopfront when it comes to getting guest appearances on radio and television. Keep it up to date, especially around the time you are pitching. And always have a good profile shot and cover image. Have one of you looking professional. This speaks volumes when a show's producer is looking to book a new guest for their show.

CHAPTER 17
LAUNCH TIME

As a journalist, I attended countless launches. Some were memorable for good reasons and others left me feeling like I wasted my time. One of the first major launches I attended as a journalist was when pop singer Shane Filan from the band Westlife (hugely popular in the 90s and 2000s) opened a clothes shop in his hometown of Sligo, Ireland. Crowds queued outside for hours beforehand. There was PR done before the launch that tied in with Shane loving his hometown and wanting to give something back. His new business venture was located in what was his parents' former business premises, a fast-food takeaway, where Shane worked before he became a successful singer in one of the world's biggest boybands. There were many angles to the story, and it was covered locally and nationally. There was a live piece done to camera for a television show. And of course, Shane was there to give interviews and pose for photographs with fans. People went away happy and some even bought clothes. A highly successful launch was had.

But how do you replicate that when you are starting from scratch and don't have any media pulling power? You have to think first about what kind of launch you want and what type of special guest is suitable, or if you even need anyone. Will you be enough to be both the master of ceremonies and the guest? The answer should always be yes. This is because you know your business inside and out. Starting off, you are your best spokesperson, and as you grow, you can add celebrities into the mix. A launch is a huge event for any business.

But before you think about themes, colours, venues (online and offline), invite list(s), drinks, and canapes, you need to think seriously about **why you are having a launch**. Launches are a lot of work and you will find yourself burning the midnight oil many times before launch day. Not only that, but you also need to have a strategy built around your launch, so you are maximising it to its utmost. If the launch is for your business, you should have a product or service to feature alongside this. You should look at having something significant for people to purchase on the spot or order online or donate to. People and the press will need something to focus on, something they can get their "teeth" into as well as your business story. Also, the launch should be about the wider picture of the business, its roots, ethos, background, and future ambitions.

One of the most important things to have set up and tested at least twice beforehand is the customer journey to purchase. What happens when a potential customer comes to your site? What happens if they leave without taking action? Think about the journey you want to take them on, so that they purchase from you with ease. As you can see, there is a lot to think about before you go about organising the details of the launch event itself. I won't be going into details about wine and food in this chapter, but there are other important aspects you need to consider.

Launch timing

Plan your calendar carefully around when you want to do your launch. Decide whether a weekend or weekday suits best. Think about those you are inviting. Does a weekend suit them best, for example, if they have to travel? Would you feel more comfortable having a full day away from the distractions of the office for your launch? Or does having a morning at home on a Saturday and going straight into launch mode in the afternoon sound better to you and your guests? You could offer a Saturday afternoon like no other to your guests and include some kind of relaxation element or a pampering session. And if you don't want any distractions from the office on the day, a weekend might be a better option. That is just one consideration.

You also need to consider the type of media you want to target and whether you feel certain that your launch will be of major interest to them. Ideally, you will have already told them about it, following the same guidelines as you would for sending in a press release as you will be using the Launch Press Release type I mentioned in a previous chapter about the types of press releases. You'll know their deadlines and will work to suit those you can accommodate. Days and weeks before your launch, you will be following up with them and sending reminders.

But don't try to accommodate everyone, as this is just not possible. Concentrate on getting a good launch first and foremost, and the press will want to cover it regardless. Also, it is in your best interests to not have all the coverage happen in all the press outlets at once. Yes, it is good to get coverage on the day and in the days/weeks/months before, but it is also great to get coverage one to two weeks later, or even months later to keep momentum going and to keep your name in the press for longer and over a sustained period.

Check your date against the dates of other major events. This is huge. Don't clash with other major events in your area, especially with longstanding ones. They are around a lot longer than your launch and they happen every year, so you are already putting yourself up against tough competition if you plan your launch around the same time as these events. I once got an invite for a launch on the same day as an election! I shouldn't have to tell you that a journalist will not choose your launch before an election. On another occasion, a wedding shop opened its doors on the same day that a major bridal event was taking place in another part of town, attracting practically all its potential customers, thus leading to a very underwhelming launch crowd.

In short, you should know what is happening around you before booking your launch. Know what festivals are on in your area and not just locally, look further afield too. If you are launching a sports product and a major sports final is on that same day, you are going to find it hard get attention unless you are going to try to link into it (you would need a great idea). Also, going up against other longstanding events sends out a bad vibe and you never know when down the line you might like to collaborate on something, and you don't want to start on the wrong foot by going straight into competitive mode with your first launch.

Mark out all the times of year when major holidays are on like Easter, Christmas, Bank Holidays, and any other days where people are likely to be distracted. Also, remember that having a launch too close to Christmas makes it hard for people to get out of the festive rush and into something else. Other days to cross off are Valentine's Day (unless it is relevant to your business), St Patrick's Day (in Ireland and other countries who celebrate this in a major way like the US and the UK, or similar national holidays if you are based in another country), Christmas Day, New Year's Eve and New Year's Day. Also, double-check that the day you've chosen doesn't coincide with a commemoration of a time in history like Memorial Day or Independence Day. If you find out that it does clash with a major event and you cannot change it, figure out a way of incorporating it if you can. It can come across that you planned it this way!

Staging events at times of the year when media outlets are not terribly busy, especially in August, can work. This is when most government meetings, courts, inquests, and other government agency meetings close down (sometimes for all the summer months). But make sure not to clash with major summer festivals. Do your research and pick a date wisely. Most importantly, pick one that suits you. Whatever you do, don't go too early with your launch date, and put yourself under huge pressure unless you really have to. Launches are stressful enough without adding tight deadlines to it.

Then, there are things you can't control. Like the time a traffic accident prevented people from getting to a launch because fire brigades and ambulances had to deal with the injured. Events like this can sometimes have surprisingly good results. In the case of a shooting that happened close to where a ceramics business had literally just opened, this ended up being a huge story. A case of bad timing and bad luck, you might think. In the end, it turned out to be a great media story for the business. A television crew that came to cover the shooting did a small piece to camera with the business owner asking him questions about what it was like when the shots went off and what he did to protect his customers inside the shop at the time. Weeks later a lifestyle show did a 15-minute segment on the business. Radio stations were also clambering for quotes from the business owner. Who has the terrible luck of opening their business on the same day there is a shooting dead of a man in broad daylight on the same street? People talked about it for a long time after, and the business became a talking point on the back of its bad luck.

Some ways of doing this include having a commemorative photo at reception, a flag, a short video playing – something that recognises that you knew all along that it is a special day in history. If someone major in your city is associated with this day, you could incorporate this into your launch or welcome speech. It is your way of acknowledging this, and it will be remembered by those who attend.

Launch venue – physical or online

Ideally, you would have your launch in your business premises. But what if your business premises is tiny or you would like to have it in a hotel or unique launch venue like a lighthouse or beach hut so you can offer an "experience" at your launch that attendees will remember. Look close to home before moving out of your business premises for the launch. You want to bring people to your door so always do a checklist of what is good and not so good about your own business premises before you decide to go outside it for your launch.

Look at various constructs you could do for your launch stage. Where are things like electrical sockets, the Wi-Fi box? How many seats could the venue space hold? Or will people be standing? Is it a comfortable space for people to mingle or will they be inclined to leave once the launch is over? Do you want a morning or evening launch? Or both? To suit different sections of your audiences. Does that matter to you? If you do decide to go to a different venue, try to team up with them instead of just hiring the venue and not communicating to them what you are doing. Venues are always happy to promote events so allow them to help you in a way that makes things easy for you.

If you are sticking to an online launch, then there are lots you can do that give it that "experience" feeling. To help guests mingle, you can have themed break out rooms in your online event. These can be topics that are relevant to your business right now and inside you can have an expert or someone from your business chairing that room. You can broadcast your launch from your place of business. For this, I always recommend setting up a main area or stage that is the main focus point for viewers. Look at it as a "back to the studio" type of space which acts as the anchor for your launch event. Here you will have your main presenter and it is where you will interview any guests, hosts reading (for a book launch), host debates on topics.

If you can afford it, it is great to have an image reel running on a screen in the background that highlights your business. Here too, you can put up comments or questions from attendees so they can be answered by the panel. As a surprise for guests, it is a good idea to send them a small token online (it could be a voucher or a ticket to something you are hosting in the future) as a thank you and to keep the conversation going.

Have influencers present who you have affiliate agreements with so they will be inclined to post to social media about the launch right throughout the event. You may think that having it online doesn't require as much work as a physical launch. But it does! You'll need help in the form of moderators, group leaders and someone good with technical issues as they can be hard to cope with during the launch as well as doing everything else.

However, the best thing is that you can keep a very tight control over your launch and call time on it, so you stick to your timetable. This isn't so easy to manage when you have a large group at a venue.

How one business made their tiny venue work for them

For me, a launch is all about the experience. I went to the launch of a tiny pub once that was once a butcher's. It was a long, narrow space. The pub's owners decided to keep the past of the building alive by having old pictures of its previous owner on the walls and keeping some old memorabilia like a weighing scales and the glass cupboards that were used to store meat. The counter was refurbished, but it was the same one that stood there for over 60 years. People liked that the bar wasn't turned into something they didn't recognise. There was respect for what had gone before. The props also made for good photos.

And instead of having everyone come at once, they staggered their launch throughout the whole day. Groups of people arrived at allocated times and got to sample some wine and finger food and were treated to a short half-hour video show about the business that was peppered with some behind the scenes footage of the fit-out, remarks from the previous owner, the work on the pub and some good luck messages and memories from locals and celebrities. People went away having "experienced" the launch. As well as sampling some food and drink, they got to learn about the business, its owners, background, the work they put into it and also got to hear some funny stories. Thus, they were likely to talk about it and about the business. And it was automatically associated with a satisfying, positive experience.

What could have proved disastrous would have been to have the guests squeezed together at the one time in a tiny bar. The organisers thought about all the logistics and adapted their launch accordingly. The guests didn't talk about how tiny the place was. They talked about how great the launch was. So, even if your business venue is tiny, you can do the same. You can stagger your launch over an entire day. You can split groups into categories. You could have local political figures in one group, a local exercise group in another, an elderly group in another. These groups will be happy that you put some thought into getting them together. They will be happy to attend the launch and to catch up with each other or make new friends.

There are a lot of logistics involved in this kind of opening, and you might just want to open the doors at the one time and get on with it. That is fine too, once you are offering some kind of experience when your visitors get inside. Because if you don't give some thought to the type of experience you want people to have, you are missing your opportunity to get in front of an already captive audience and impress them. Word of mouth remains one of the most trusted ways to generate interest and influence.

Special guest

There is so much to consider before booking a special guest. I've included everything important for you from a media publicity perspective, so you feel prepared before you go ahead and book someone. Make a list of those within and outside of your niche. If you are thinking of booking a special guest, you should start a list of those who would fit your launch best. It could be someone from your field or someone outside your field who brings something a little special. It could be the latest reality tv star or a famous YouTuber. Just make sure that you know a lot about them and do plenty of research. Get this information from them, their agent, their social media feed, any reviews, and any press clippings. See what they have said before in interviews and posted online on various topics. Then see if this ties in with or goes against what you are trying to convey. Also, see if they have done any launches before. And if they have, then this is a golden ticket for you to find out what they were like. Go ask the business that booked them and get details. Ideally, get on a phone call with the organiser, that way you will get more information by the tone of voice they use to describe how the guest was.

Make a list of between 5 and 10. Test their relevancy and for those outside of your niche, look at what they could bring that would be different and surprising to attendees. Don't just book a celebrity without knowing if they have an interest in what you do or have said anything concerning what you do/or in your area. If your guest doesn't have a genuine interest either before or during your talks around booking them, he/she will need a lot more coaching from you ahead of any interviews with the press. You will need to figure time into doing this and you may not have a lot especially when you get the guest's schedule and realize that there isn't even time for a few Zoom calls.

Do your research. Don't book a guest who has said something controversial that could be tied into your business. The press may try to reignite an old controversial story and link it to your's if they can. Booking the guest that said controversial comments in the past is enough for some media. The story might read "Their special guest is John Smith who previously said that…." Of course, unless you want to use this previous controversy point as part of your publicity, then you would need to map out a strategy around this. Also be aware that if you are going with someone controversial, your launch may not be the most important thing to a press person. The controversy will always win out and your business launch may not get the most attention it deserves. You don't want your launch to be dominated by comments your special guest said the week before. While these comments might bring more publicity to your event, at the end of the day, the celebrity will be the main focus, and not what they are there to do. Your product or service may just get lost amongst it all.

Spokesperson potential

Ask yourself would you be happy with having this person talk about your business before, during and long after the launch is over? Would you be happy if they were asked a question a year from now, and would you be confident that they could answer it? You also need to determine whether you are happy with this person being the front person for your business for the launch day and for many months and even years after. Oftentimes, people go with someone who already works in media, like a tv presenter or an actor. And while it is a safe and good idea, let me tell you a story that is slightly different.

An elderly lady performed the honours of a launch I attended. She was the oldest woman living in the area and she had worked in the business for several years before it had undergone this transformation that everyone was there to help launch. She gave a passionate speech at the launch and it resonated well with the press. She wasn't a celebrity. She wasn't well experienced at public speaking. But what she had was passion, knowledge, and the ability to deliver. It got the business a huge amount of publicity from all kinds of angles. They were applauded for allowing her to perform the launch. It proved they were not ageist and didn't need a hot young model or media celebrity to do the job. It also proved that they were in tune with what was going on around them. They knew about this woman and she was well-liked and known in the area.

Think long-term

Think long-term when you are booking a special guest. The photos with this person will travel far and wide on social media and you will want this impression to gather momentum and have a short-term impact on social media, but also a longer-term impact in terms of brand promotion. You might also want to use these photos as part of your future branding and for other press stories you may want to pitch for.

Contract/Agreement

Firstly, I want to say that I am not a lawyer so get legal advice on this if you have any doubts. Having a contract or agreement is vital. Even if the guest or the guest's agent is slow at doing this, get something in writing or in an email. All the terms should be laid down in writing. You need confirmation of what is acceptable and not acceptable before your launch. You also need to know what you can use afterwards.

Yes, there will be some negotiations when you have a special guest, but compromising is key here to a certain extent but always remind yourself of why you are booking this person. If at any stage, things go off-course, then make a decision to not go ahead with the negotiations, save yourself a headache and stress and find another special guest.

Key things to ask and put in a contract/email/agreement

Get down to the nitty-gritty details. If you have a guest person coming to launch your business or product, make sure you have thorough talks about what he or she can and, more importantly, cannot do. I have turned up to launches with a photographer and when I ask the organiser can the special guest do this or that, they don't know.

Know exactly what the guest will do. Get some information and statistics on any previous coverage a special guest has achieved for a business. Get these stats beforehand so you know exactly what you are paying for. Right before the launch, double check the contract/agreement you have. Oftentimes, emails over and back will change things slightly and an agent may agree to something and forget to update the contract. Make sure you have the most up to date one.

Are you paying all up front or half before and half after? This is an important detail as some are insistent on full payment beforehand. This may impact on what you can afford depending on your cashflow for the launch. If you have someone in mind and you know exactly what you want, then state this in your earliest conversations. Also, make it known that you feel your launch could help the special guest get back in the media.

You may already know that the special guest you are looking for may not be as popular as they once were, and you can try to use this but being fair is important. You may also find that when you book a celebrity 6 months in advance, which I recommend you do if they are a major celebrity, the absolute minimum being 4-5 months, they could become hugely popular in the intervening time or fall off the radar media-wise. Make sure you secure a fitting price before you begin, and do not leave anything unanswered if it is a case that you haven't set a price early on (Again, get some professional advice on this).

Get a short video, testimonial, and the terms with which you can use this material. Always include that you want a testimonial from the guest celebrity in the contract, one you can use for a time afterward (if that is allowed). Make sure you get the exact testimonial in writing and on video or audio and have it date-stamped and agreed on that you can use it indefinitely or for a certain period. Also, you will need to know exactly where you can use it: your website, your flyers, etc.

I urge you to get the finer details in writing. And don't be afraid to list out exactly what has been agreed on and ask the agent to clarify that this is all correct. Also, get a short video from the special guest that you can use on all your platforms prior to the launch. Give the guest a script that he/she can follow. Include in this, things like what they are doing at your event, how he or she is looking forward to it, and have them say why your audience should come along. This is a great way to get the word out about your event prior to the day itself. Have specific terms laid out on how you can use this video, so everyone is clear, and no one is unhappy when it starts popping up on all platforms and on media sites.

Future photo use and follow-on

You should also ask if the guest will be happy to use photos as part of future promotions that are relevant along with the testimonial. Also, find out if the special guest might do an interview six months to a year later as part of a follow-on piece. Oftentimes, press outlets are looking for follow-on pieces and if your business still has a strong connection with this special guest, then this is a story that you can capitalise on. You can pitch the story as a year's recap on what's happened in your business. You will be reminding the press that you brought a certain celebrity to town and that this person has remained supportive of your business. It is often the case that special guests turn up and leave after a few hours and you never hear from him/her again.

So, if you can persuade him/her to remain in touch, it could be incredibly good for both of you. You can also ask if it would be possible for the special guest to come back and pay your business a visit a year or two years from now. This can be difficult to achieve, and the guest won't be too keen to do this unless you have a close bond. In a year, a lot might have changed for this celebrity. They make have landed a major role and by still being in touch, you will benefit from their added celebrity status.

Get insights from the talent agent

As you go through your list and contact agents, ask the agent about any up-and-coming people they have on their books. This is a good time to build a relationship early. You can be the one who gives this person a start in publicity by hiring them for your business. Always remember that you are the one offering the opportunity. Go in with this attitude, and it will change how you are seen by talent agents. You are the one providing media opportunities by having a launch, and this is important to keep in mind. Also, keep an eye on television guests who are doing small segments on shows like say presenting a lifestyle segment, the cooking slot, or the weather. They will typically be happy to help you, won't cost as much as a major celebrity but will have good publicity skills and be somewhat well known among the public.

The launch itself

You should give yourself at the very least 4-6 months of a lead-in time for a launch. if your main press outlets are major magazines and supplements, then, 6-8 months is the absolute minimum as some of these go to print very early. For a magazine issue in September, you would need to be ready to pitch out for publicity in February. And you may need more time if you are booking a special guest from the top tier as you will need to match up your schedules. The very minimum in this scenario is 7-8 months.

I always encourage, if possible, that if this is your first major launch you should start having conversations and brainstorming out ideas with colleagues, collaborators, photographers, and any others involved at least 11 months beforehand. Begin to put a publicity plan together shortly after this and factor in deadlines for each step.

Having a minimum of 8 months gives you enough time to draw up your contract with your guest, have meetings with the venue, pitch to outlets, revise pitches, get photos, organise photocalls, set up affiliates, get a core group to champion your launch get your collateral organised, lighting, canapes, drinks, speeches, and welcome packs if you are having any. I believe invitees should have something to carry away with them. Such takeaway packs can include details about your business and some products from you or from partners that they can try. But make sure you put some effort into the packs. People and journalists even more so are used to getting packs at launches, especially members of the press. I had a collection of pens, mugs, t-shirts, and posters from all the launches I went to. Look at adding something uniquely memorable to your business pack. Something personal to each journalist is always a nice touch. Rather than the same mug to everyone, why not write a headline from a story from each journalist on their mug instead. Or use this as the text on a t-shirt. You could champion your charity in your t-shirts.

Having a memorable launch is what it is all about

Example: I got a client of mine to get her 13-year-old daughter (who is an accomplished painter) to design her launch invites, a welcome card for her goodie bag and a welcome poster. The launch invite was printed on a t-shirt for all the goodie bags. As well as being the talk of the event, the business got a lot of publicity on the back of this alone. It was a family business and including her designs was a really lovely touch, and the daughter was delighted (and don't worry, she was paid for her efforts!).

At your launch, people must have something to do, look at, hear and/or watch. Don't have people simply stand around and then assume that they will chat amongst each other. People who go to launches by themselves and journalists are almost always by themselves though sometimes with a photographer, will chit-chat with others. But there will come a point when they feel uncomfortable about doing this. They won't do it for an hour or two hours. People who go alone will be more likely to stay longer if things are happening at your launch. And not just the speeches! Members of the press are used to standing around, and they almost expect this at a launch. But the longer they wait for things to start and happen, the more they start to regret going. There are a million events that members of the press can go to. So, if you can get them there, make sure they are being informed, can do their job by getting the interviews they need and leave feeling like it was worth their time attending.

Having a **press section** is a good idea so you can have someone from your team meet and greet the journalists, give them information, tell them about the run of events and set up interviews. Have the area decorated so any social media posts/interviews, live interviews for tv and any type of publicity has your company banner or logo in the background. If possible, have it well-lit for influencers and photographers who will want to get well composed images. If it is a make-up launch, for example, have the journalists try some make-up on.

If it's a service, then have someone lined up for them to interview who has a good knowledge of it. Have the special guest prepped for interviews and have a timetable where each journalist gets an allocated time with the person. Or host a press conference where all the journalists can ask questions. Have the special guest work with the press, pose for photos, drum up some excitement, give a talk, or present a segment. Have props at your event that people can take photos at and post on social media. These can be posters, cut-outs, a video your special guest recorded prior to the event. Maximise this content. Have this video playing at the entrance to the event as well as on your social media platforms and in your email marketing.

Having pop up stalls is an excellent way to walk visitors and journalists through an experience. You have say 3-4 stalls where each one details a different part of your business or product. Have them laid out in such a way that one part follows the other. You will find that visitors and journalists tend to gravitate towards these things because they like to have something to do at a launch and telling all attendees about your business in an engaging way when you have an engaged audience is the best time to do it. You can include in these stalls things like testimonials from previous clients or big-name customers or a person that is well known in your area. Think about the layout of your launch venue. Having things spread out across your launch venue is best. People are not all huddled together on one side of the room listening to one person or at the other side at stalls. Guide them through the experience by literally having them go from place to place. That way you can really tell your story in an engaging way.

There are plenty of launch venue experts that can help you with the storytelling around your launch and in particular your launch venue. I encourage you to look at the whole thing as an experience and not just focus on the stage where your guest speakers will talk. Look at it from a visitor's point of view getting to know you for the first time. What would you want them to know? And more importantly, what would you like them to remember? Also, remember this all goes for journalists too. Having various elements to the launch taps into that part of their brain that asks how many stories can I get from this one launch? If they can get more than one story, then their time will be of huge value to their publication and the stories they get will prove to their editor that it was worth their time and effort away from the desk to get these interesting stories. The launch should have a feel-good vibe to it. It is exciting for you as a business owner. This excitement should seep out of everything that is part of the launch. If you can, this excitement could have a surprise element. Whether this is a part of the takeaway pack or is delivered as a big reveal at the launch, it should be something you think about with your audience in mind.

Here are some ideas to consider:

You could keep the identity of the celebrity secret

Your special guest could be your big reveal, but you will need to drum up publicity without using the person's name. This is done at times by major companies, but if you are starting out, it wouldn't be recommended, as you need this person to get publicity, and announcing the identity of your special guest is the best way of doing this. However, if you want to try it and think you have the time and ideas to put this into action, it is not impossible to drum up good publicity by keeping the identity of your celebrity a secret. Let's look at how you could do this in an exciting way.

- *Treasure Hunt*
You can work with a local newspaper or radio to run a competition to see if anyone can guess the guest's name by using clues. You could do a treasure hunt around your town or city and see who pieces the clues together. You can drip feed content on your site or blog. Or get a local newspaper to run a photo of the person and reveal a new part each week. There are lots of ways but try to make it intriguing and fun. That way, people won't get bored, and you will drum up excitement over a certain period. If you are doing this, you could have the winner meet your special guest for a 1-1 session or tea or a drink as part of their prize. This is a particularly nice gesture

if the special guest is someone very well known (remember, you need to put this in the terms and conditions of booking them in advance).

- Run a competition
Run a competition for a prize that is connected to your launch. If you want to drum up some major publicity, you could offer a high-value prize and link in with newspapers, radio, and television to get coverage. You can run adverts at times when your ideal audience is listening (Get stats about figures beforehand from the advertising agents).

Don't delay the start time

Start no later than 10 minutes after the scheduled launch time. I've attended events where they started one or two hours after the stated launch time, and this is unacceptable. The longest you can expect someone to stay at your launch is an hour, maybe two hours. So, starting this late means you will have people leave and talk about your launch in a negative way. And those that do stay on will have lost interest and will be looking to leave once they can. If your special guest is running extremely late, instead of hiding it from people for fear of being embarrassed, just tell them, be up-front and try to offer something else to entertain them. Start with something else on the programme. Have the launch timed out in section. The introduction to the launch, the main launch event, and the wrap-up. Try not to let the event lag too much. Get those involved into position and have them as excited as you are. If it is a simple launch, it's best to think of it as being an hour long, with some mingling after the event for 30-45 minutes. Make sure you have discussed with the venue the possibility that the launch might run over and ensure that the venue isn't booked for another event after yours.

CHAPTER 18
DEALING WITH EMOTIONS AND MEDIA PUBLICITY

Going on a journey to get media publicity can be an emotional rollercoaster. And this side of things is rarely talked about if ever. I know that dealing with the many emotions you will experience on this journey can be exasperating and mentally exhausting. One minute you are being asked on regularly by a radio show. The next you stop hearing from them, and you wonder what you did wrong. You feel you have sufficient coverage locally to merit pitching to a national newspaper but after three attempts you hear nothing back. And you feel like giving up. This is just the tip of the iceberg. This is why I felt it was important to include a chapter about this in this book.

Confidence

Confidence is a complicated emotion. On the one hand, you want to come across like you know what you are talking about but on the other, you don't want to come across as overly confident or aloof. I remember when I did my first live television interview. It was a music slot for a daytime Irish programme, and I was brought on to talk about a Westlife show that was happening and their new album. I had written about Westlife for years and I felt I would be able to answer almost any questions about the band. Their new album had a song written by two of the band members, which was a new development in the band's career.

The interview was going well and then came the singalong part. This was a surprise to me. And a shock. I was going to have to sing along and fill in the blanks of certain lyrics of songs. The camera captured my shocked face (which they showed to everyone again at the end of my segment and used it in other parts of the show too). I have a very expressive face, so I'm told. But I went with the flow, I had to, not having any choice. But my initial face was one of utter shock. I could have reacted badly to this and said I don't sing, or I can't sing. But I laughed it off (once my shocked face disappeared!) and went with it and it turned out to be a bit of a laugh. It also helped take my mind off the cameras.

I was at first worried about what viewers would think but after the first one or two songs, I was enjoying myself and this came across. My confidence was higher because I just went with the flow and trusted that I could do it. When you let go a little bit and become a little less tense and forget the cameras, your true personality comes through and your confidence soars. I share this experience because it taught me a lot straight out of the gate. It taught me about the importance of preparation and being generally knowledgeable around your subject area. It shows that you are an interesting person and someone others would like to have a coffee with if you are comfortable being put on the spot and showing you can laugh at yourself. If you can show the presenters, the researchers, and the audience that you can have a laugh then you will be remembered and considered for future appearances before the person who just couldn't let go and go with the flow.

Knockbacks

Dealing with the media can be tough. There are a lot of knockbacks and a lot of replies like the standard "we didn't have room for it this week", which translates to "it wasn't good enough". When you go to pitch for the first time and you feel you need to make a follow-up email about your story, have notes ready like the following:

- When you sent it in and who you sent it to
- What the main angle of the story is
- Where it is suited to in the paper (but mention that you are happy if it is included someplace else)
- Whether it has photos (what kind of photos is important too)
- When the event is happening – a deadline
- Always ask if there is anything else a journalist needs

Having a summary to hand will allow you to be less nervous especially when you decide that you need to call the newsroom/journalist. You will come across so much better when you ring a busy newsroom and the journalist on the other end is letting you know purely by their tone of voice that he/she doesn't have time to look through dozens of emails to find your one. They can decide purely by the summary you are about to give them. Try to remain friendly even though their tone of voice may sound to you like they would rather be anywhere else except talking to you. Before you make this call, please read the segment in Chapter 6 "To Call or Not To Call".

Worry

Clients I've worked with talk a lot about worrying that either they or the media will do a bad job. "They won't understand my story" or "I'll mess it all up" or "I'm no good at these things." Businesses that are worried about dealing with the press for the first time should start with something small. I suggest one of the following:

The announcement of a new staff member: this includes their photo and short bio of them. These get featured in the business sections of local newspapers and on radio business shows.
Host a small charity event in the office: take some photos yourself or hire a photographer to take them and send them in with a small story to go along with it.
Leverage other events: If you as the business owner or your CEO is going to an event, have them get their photo taken at it with others or with the main speaker and send that in with a short caption.
Personal milestones: Are you as the business owner or your CEO celebrating a wedding anniversary, getting married, having a first child, having twins or triplets? You can see about getting a photo taken and sending that in with a short caption.

These are ways that you can introduce yourself to members of the press and know that not too much can go wrong in these types of scenarios. They are small ways to get started and can be a genuine way to connect with journalists. They will also build your confidence and combat worry when dealing with the media. You can grow your media pitch in small steps starting off with any of the above, then moving on to a pitch email, a press release, a photocall, a launch. Grow it at your own pace.

Why face-to-face is important

If you think you may be dealing mainly with the same person when you seek coverage in your local newspaper, then it is good to try to build a relationship and get to know him or her. Sports companies are particularly good at this and they invite sports editors to various events throughout the year like award shows, announcements of new players, and managers to build relationships face-to-face.

You can invite a journalist into your business or invite them along to an event you are hosting for other business leaders in your area. It is harder these days to get a journalist out of the newsroom because when they are not working on a story for print, they are working on one for the website or dealing with social media. So, you need to make it worth their while to leave the office. Initially, it is a good idea to get them onto a 10-minute online call so you can do a meet and greet and then can ask questions. It is not always easy to meet face-to-face but when possible, you should make the effort.

Uncertainty - change of reporter

If the person you normally deal with changes, send a quick email to their replacement telling them a bit about you and how you are there to help. This is a really important email because this person is new and will be looking for stories and to make connections. The person they replaced may have left little or no handover notes so they could literally be starting from scratch. Even that doesn't stop editors from asking them for stories or angles. You'll be happy you sent them this email because you are acknowledging that they have just started, and you will be introducing yourself to them at a time when they may need you most. You are also preventing any roadblocks that can come your way when a new reporter takes over.

The journalist may want to start afresh and generate their own contacts. You don't want to be banging your head off a brick wall especially if you have just started to get publicity in this media outlet. Get in there early with a friendly email and introduce yourself and outline your expertise. You may find that they get back to your email very quickly as they are looking for leads and may ask you if you have anything interesting to share. This is your chance to pitch an eager journalist so go for it! You can ask to meet them for coffee sometime as meeting new journalists face-to-face helps you to build your confidence and you will get better insights into how best to work with them.

Stamina and consistency

Once you start on your media journey, the only way to build your confidence and the confidence of journalists is by pitching stories. Don't worry if your first pitch isn't very good, pitch again, and again. If you still don't get anywhere, ask or invite them to an event you are going to. Talk to them and ask if there is anything you can help them with. You might get a short answer to start with but let them know about your expertise and let it sit with them for a while. You will find that given time they will be back on to you looking for your expertise for a story they are writing.

If you are struggling to get anywhere and you feel like giving up, don't. Try the power of the piggy-back/newsjacking/Reactive PR, which is a trick I get many clients to do when they are starting. It works like this: Can you piggyback on a story that is making the headlines? Can you align yourself with another organisation that has gotten coverage in the past? Can you piggy-back on their coverage to start with? Can you do an event together and send in a press release about your new partnership? Basically, ask yourself – can you piggy-back and make yourself relevant to a story that is ongoing in the media right now? Tailor your pitch/photo/press release to this angle.

When you feel like this is not working, I encourage you to hire a photographer to take some fun shots at Halloween or Valentine's

Day or another time of year that is important for your business. Caption them and send them in with a short story. Maybe your press release doesn't have any bite, but no one has told you this. If it is not getting picked up by anyone, then you should hire someone to have a look at it and make it better (I help write and edit press releases and pitch emails). If they suggest something controversial, be sure you are confident enough to stand over your stance. Take a look at how you can create something in your business that would attract attention. Could you support a new or controversial cause? Could you start a research project into a certain element of your business sector (make sure you get a reputable company to collate data for you), could you do some videos of how you help clients and get some client testimonials?

By putting your mind into getting media publicity and by being more media aware, you'll start to see what works. Ideas will come to you by being immersed in the area. You'll be listening to shows, watching shows, and reading media publications. It will start to come together, trust me, it will. The more you pitch, the easier it will be to deal with rejection and confidence issues as you can revert to your story list and pick another idea (or look at the Idea Generation chapter) and start again. If you find after three separate attempts that you are still finding it hard, then I feel you need to reach out for help. Don't keep struggling alone. One tip from someone could change your whole viewpoint and give you the breakthrough you need. Don't sit and ruminate. Reach out.

What happens when the journalist makes a mistake?

A journalist, like anyone else, can make an honest mistake. It sometimes happens, and unless you deal with it directly and with some determination, you may find that a newspaper may be slow to do something about it especially if it doesn't defame you in any way. But this is causing you a lot of stress and as a business owner you need to get it corrected as soon as possible.

If the journalist has made a mistake, this is what I suggest you do next: Print out the article or cut it out of the physical issue leaving the date on the page and also cut out the front page. Or save a link to the page and also take a screenshot with the date of publication clearly visible. Get your details correct and have them ready for when you go to contact the journalist.

- Clearly outline your reason for wanting/needing this to be corrected, indicating what impact it will have on your business and reputation if it isn't corrected.
- Include details of what kind of reaction you would like from the media outlet but also have one drafted should they ask for a response there and then that they need to show their editor. If you feel you need a solicitor, contact him/her before you contact the journalist so you can use this in your conversation should the need arise.
- So, the time comes to make the call or send in an initial email. I always recommend an email first but the exception to this is if that mistake is a major one. Then, I always say make that call as soon as you can.
- Contact the journalist who wrote the piece and outline your reasons for needing the mistake corrected.
- Often, a correction is offered straightaway. You can ask for it to be early on in the newspaper, like Page 1 (if it was a really terrible mistake) or Page 3 or 5. However, you may not get a say in this. Editors know though that a mistake rectified on page 54 isn't going to be good enough. Sometimes, it is common for mistakes to be corrected in the same section that the original article was published or the

- same slot that the original piece was broadcast.
- You can ask that the outlet donates to a charity of your choice to make up for the error.
- You can ask for another interview to be done when you are launching something new (you might prefer another journalist to do it next time).
- Make sure whatever you agree to is sufficient. I have seen companies go in with a complaint and be told to get lost. But they later come back with more information about the impact the mistake has had on their business, and they then get an apology or correction.
- Mistakes that put your business in jeopardy need to be corrected, simple as that.

Most journalists are happy to correct mistakes and they will be done promptly. There may also be a need to keep the correction up online for a certain period too. Having open and constructive discussions with the journalist or editor will help to get the issue resolved quickly and will minimise any fallout in your relationship. Your level of reaction should somewhat equate to the level of mistake (I know this can be hard at the time and especially when the mistake is out in the newspaper or has been broadcast and is online). However, think long term and try to see this as a way of dealing with the situation as quickly and effectively as possible and showing that you are someone that understands that mistakes can be made.

Know that whatever emotion you are experiencing is one that someone else is or has experienced too. Trust that you are on this journey for a reason and that rejection is a normal part of the process that eventually leads to doors opening and abundance flowing in your direction. You just have to believe in the journey.

CHAPTER 19

CONCLUSION and MEDIA PUBLICITY CHECKLIST

Becoming a press go-to person is the ultimate aim of any businessperson or personality. This is when the press is seeking you out, not the other way around. Any time there is something remotely connected to what you do, and most importantly if you are as they say in the industry "good for a quote" or an interview, you will have truly earned your position in the media. This comes with hard work, stamina, and consistency. So don't expect this any time quick. When it does happen, you should treat yourself. When you become this go-person, there are a few things I would like to let you know about.

It comes with perks and downsides. Oftentimes you might be called at any time for a quote or to come into the studio at short notice. When I was a full-time journalist, I was always on the lookout for go-to people I could rely on for various topics and for things I needed at the last minute. Politics, Health, Education, Crime, Technology, Lifestyle, Make-up. I updated my contacts list on a twice-yearly basis, considering how reliable and topical each person was and whether it was time to get a new go-to person in a certain field. Also, a go-to person needs to be available at any time, and this may not be possible for you. Anyone I contacted three times but wasn't able to get a quote from or some kind of response was removed from my list. Also, there is an onus on the media to not have the same person quoted all the time. Hence, the need to change the list often.

Audiences know when they see a name too often and that can put them off a publication or broadcast. It can feel too cozy or too familiar. But if a journalist finds that someone special who resonates with viewers and listeners, then the public associates that person with that outlet, and that is good for everyone. By hearing their voice or reading their opinion, they know that it is a certain radio show, programme, or newspaper that they are consuming and enjoying. And that, for members of the media, is gold. You will find on radio and television in particular that they have go-to people that relate well to their audience in a live setting.

When to say no

If you are being asked on to a show and are starting to become a go-to person, then you will need to know when to say no. It is easy to say yes all the time. But this can be dangerous if you are not ready for the topic at hand. If you feel you are out of your depth on a subject or don't want to get involved in a certain topic, it is okay to say no. Don't feel like you will be missing out on future opportunities by saying no. Actually, by saying no and explaining why (not being knowledgeable enough or having a conflict of interest are two examples), you will gain more respect.

I worked on a show previously and we were having a guest on who was just back from holidays when a big political story had just broken. It was right up his street and we got ready to prep him and bring him on. But it turned out that he hadn't been keeping up to date with this story (he said he had) and we were left with no one to bring on at the last minute. It turned out to be less than ideal, and there was a lot of anxiety. In the end, another journalist was brought on in his place, and it luckily turned out okay in the end. But this particular guest was promoted by the programme beforehand, and one of the presenters had to hastily come up with an explanation as to why he wasn't appearing as advertised. It pays to say no if you are not ready. Don't be that person who puts pressure on the show's crew and presenters just because you couldn't say no.

Keep up to date

Staying up to speed with what is happening is vital. Say no if you feel you have been out of the loop for a bit too long, caught up in other aspects of your business or just not feeling ready. It is great if you can research quickly and get ready before going on to a show. You should congratulate yourself on being able to get ready for a television or radio show quickly. This is a skill. And remember to be friendly when you arrive. Be open to the show taking a different angle and be open to them not using you all that much. The latter has happened to plenty a guest who travels miles to a studio, only to be let speak for three minutes. You are building relationships, building rapport with audiences and try to remember that instead of focusing on how little time you got to speak.

Some final thoughts

A media journey begins not with a single step, but with a mindset that is ready to take things in a new direction. I have encountered many highly successful businesspeople and some who were not so successful over the years. Many were apprehensive about contacting media organisations, citing reasons like being afraid of what might happen or something going wrong. I can totally understand this apprehension. Seeking media coverage can create anxiety. Dealing with the media, especially when things go wrong, can be stressful.

However, you can never tell how your journey will go unless you get on the road. Publicity can set your business up for greater visibility and success, or sometimes it can fail to ignite any reaction. I believe, though, when going into this, it is best not to think about whether your story will have any impact. Write your best story; get good photos taken; be positive in your dealings with the press; and try not to be too forceful. You will be surprised at the reaction you can get. And it will lead to success for you and your business if you are ready to give it your time, dedication, and stamina.

I've seen thousands of press releases come into my inbox over the years. I always remember the terrible ones. The ones with multiple colour fonts, the ones where there are no details of who to contact, addressed to my competitor or riddled with spelling errors. I even had one written in a language I couldn't identify. (It might have been Klingon – trekkies tend to be quirky, I've noticed.) In my years of covering stories, it's the ones who are ready to take advantage of a trend or a breaking story who are the ones that get ahead of the rest. If you spot a breaking story and you feel you can contribute to it, it is up to you to decide if you want to get in on the conversation. If you read an article or hear a comment on the radio that you disagree with, you should ask yourself if it is a good idea to respond to it from a place of knowledge. There are ways of drumming up publicity for yourself if you want to take that step. But in these scenarios, you need to be able to take it quickly.

My main advice for anyone looking for coverage is to show that you have at least read one issue or listened to/watched at least two shows prior to pitching. Sending anything in before doing this can be detrimental. Always remember too that journalists have their audience foremost in their minds. Think of the readers, the listeners, the viewers. Help them, and you help the journalist. Ultimately, of course, this helps you get steps ahead of everyone else who is pitching about their business and not considering how it is relevant to the audience of the media outlet. These pitches are the ones that only have the business or the businessperson in mind and forget about the reader. Audiences always come first. No matter what, try to remain positive. Your story might not make the news today. But, with a few tweaks, try it again or link it to something more relevant to the news agenda and your story can be news tomorrow.

Most of all - take action

Take small steps every day to get closer to getting featured. These small steps and actions will build up to being a useful resource. Watching segments of a show, listening to a radio show, reading the last two articles written by a journalist you want to contact - all of these things are small steps but when done regularly they can grow your knowledge of where you can fit in your story both now and in the future. At the time, this type of activity may seem like time wasted especially when results are not forthcoming straight away but always remember that this is a journey that you are going to take that will have lots of twists, turns, ups and downs. I encourage you to most of all start with small actions and slowly build on these once you have the time and resources to do so. Enjoy the journey and celebrate every small win.

Remember that getting featured means you managed to stand out from the hundreds of others who also pitched their story. And that is no mean feat!

Media Publicity Checklist

I know it can be daunting to start. So, I've put together this checklist so you can make sure you are ready before you send out a pitch.

1. **Online Presence** - evaluate it and be honest. Get someone neutral to evaluate it also. Does your website look inviting to a time poor journalist? Are things easy to find? Does it load quickly? Does the journalist get a sense of you straightaway on landing on the site? (Don't worry if you don't have a website, see next tip).
2. **Social Media Presence** - Same as above. Evaluate your last 5-10 posts. What were they about? Did they get much reaction? Do they align with why you want to get publicity? Your social media should speak to your media publicity efforts and act as a support player.
3. **Photos** - The last thing you want is to scramble around looking for a high-resolution photo of you or someone in your business with just minutes to go before the journalist's deadline. This happens and happens a lot. So, before you go sending off your email to a journalist, ask yourself what images do I have, what resolution are they and do I have permission to use them? Who owns them? Do these images align with what you are doing, or do you need new images?
4. **Spokesperson**: Who is going to be the front person for your campaign? I have seen campaigns with more than one but things can get confused so there is a reason why successful campaigns have one spokesperson. Spend time figuring out who is the best for the job and if they need a little training before you send them off to do interviews.
5. **Last but not least, what is your main message and what are its sub messages?** Getting this down on paper early (but being willing to adapt it as your journey grows if it aligns with what you do) is vital. This should guide you always.

About the Author

Sandra Coffey is a former journalist and editor from Ireland. She has worked in media outlets in print, broadcast and online for 17 years. She now teaches others how to get featured in the media. She and her clients have featured in Forbes, Harper's Bazaar, Closer Magazine, RTE and others. Sandra is also a fiction writer and was previously shortlisted for the Irish Short Story of the Year. See sandracoffey.com

How to work with Sandra: PR POWER HOUR

If you would like to get a taster of what it is like to work with me, then I recommend you sign up for a PR Power Hour where I can help you with an issue in your publicity and also review 500 words (max) of content. Please send content 48 hours beforehand, so I have had time to study and review it before we get on a call. Please email me at solassandra@gmail.com to book and to discuss your needs.

PUBLICITY PLANNER

Make achieving publicity so much easier by getting my publicity planner. I'm so chuffed with this planner as I feel it will make a big difference to how you plan and execute your publicity. As well as a calendar of important dates with many from across many areas of interest, I also offer advice and tips on what you should be doing during each month and what you need to do to be successful. See sandracoffey.com

LET'S CONNECT

Website: www.sandracoffey.com
Twitter: @SandraCoffey
LinkedIn:https://www.linkedin.com/in/sandra-coffey-publicitymentorandtrainer/

ACKNOWLEDGMENTS

To my parents, Leo and Una for passing on their love of news to me.

To my siblings for their never waning interest in the stories I got them to read every week. My sentences nearly always started with "have you read or heard about this?"

To my godson, Jack. You will always have a special place in my life.

I've made some wonderful friends on this journey not to mention all those I've been encouraged and inspired by in the media outlets I've worked in over the years. There are too many to mention here but I hope that this thank you serves as a way of acknowledging your influence and support throughout my career.

To the two most precious people in my life, Trevor and Nicole. Trevor's constant love, support, encouragement, and advice have been immense throughout the journey of writing this book and in our lives together. I'm forever grateful to have him by my side every day.

To my daughter, Nicole for all the joy she brings into my life. I started writing this book before she came along. Her presence has brought a new understanding of my journey as a journalist and how it has shaped who I am now. I'm so happy and grateful to have you in my life.

www.ingramcontent.com/pod-product-compliance
Lightning Source LLC
Chambersburg PA
CBHW071350210526
45465CB00001B/48